How to Use SPSS Syntax

How to Use SPSS Syntax

An Overview of Common Commands

Manfred te Grotenhuis
Chris Visscher

Radboud University Nijmegen, The Netherlands

Los Angeles | London | New Delhi
Singapore | Washington DC

Los Angeles | London | New Delhi
Singapore | Washington DC

FOR INFORMATION:

SAGE Publications, Inc.
2455 Teller Road
Thousand Oaks, California 91320
E-mail: order@sagepub.com

SAGE Publications Ltd.
1 Oliver's Yard
55 City Road
London EC1Y 1SP
United Kingdom

SAGE Publications India Pvt. Ltd.
B 1/I 1 Mohan Cooperative Industrial Area
Mathura Road, New Delhi 110 044
India

SAGE Publications Asia-Pacific Pte. Ltd.
3 Church Street
#10-04 Samsung Hub
Singapore 049483

Printed in the United States of America

Library of Congress Cataloging-in-Publication Data

Grotenhuis, Manfred te, 1967–

How to use SPSS syntax : an overview of common commands / Manfred te Grotenhuis, Chris Visscher.

pages cm
Includes bibliographical references and index.

ISBN 978-1-4833-3343-4 (pbk. : alk. paper)

1. SPSS (Computer file) 2. Social sciences—Statistical methods. I. Title.

HA32.G75 2013
005.5'5—dc23   2013031344

This book is printed on acid-free paper.

SFI label applies to text stock

Acquisitions Editor: Vicki Knight
Assistant Editor: Katie Guarino
Editorial Assistant: Jessica Miller
Production Editor: Brittany Bauhaus
Copy Editor: QuADS Prepress (P) Ltd.
Typesetter: C&M Digitals (P) Ltd.
Proofreader: Scott Oney
Cover Designer: Cristina Kubota
Marketing Manager: Nicole Elliott

14 15 16 17 10 9 8 7 6 5 4 3 2 1

Brief Contents

Detailed Contents

About the Authors

Manfred te Grotenhuis is an Assistant Professor of Quantitative Data Analysis and an affiliate of the Interuniversity Center for Social Science Theory and Methodology (ICS). He has more than 50 published articles to his credit. Some of his statistical contributions have appeared as articles in leading journals, such as *American Journal of Sociology*, *American Sociological Review*, *Journal for the Scientific Study of Religion*, and *International Journal of Epidemiology*. He has been teaching statistics at the Faculty of Social Sciences at Radboud University Nijmegen, the Netherlands, since 1995 and has written several introductory books on SPSS and statistics. He is a recipient of his university's biennial teaching award. He loves/hates to ride a 20-mile cycling time trial. He earned his Ph.D. in sociology from Radboud University Nijmegen.

Chris Visscher, with more than 30 years of teaching statistics, is a principal lecturer. In 1986, he wrote an SPSS syntax manual for students, probably the first of its kind. He is very fond of Gregorian chants and never misses an opportunity to chant, be it in the office, in church, or at students' house parties at three in the morning! He did his master's in sociology from Radboud University Nijmegen, the Netherlands.

Preface

The SPSS program (which originally stood for **S**tatistical **P**ackage for the **S**ocial **S**ciences) is one of the most commonly used statistical software packages. Due to its popularity, it is not surprising to find many SPSS textbooks available nowadays. In almost all these books, however, the emphasis is on the many SPSS menus. Clearly, the advantage of using menus is ease of use, although not all of SPSS's capacities are accessible this way. Furthermore, no record is kept of the commands executed via the menu's buttons, meaning that replicating statistical work is difficult, and it is also very hard to check what was done in the first place. This is especially troubling when something has gone (awfully) wrong. For these reasons, more skilled SPSS users store all of their work in so-called syntax files. By doing so, one is able to not only replicate and check but also make full use of the large variety of tools within the program. The makers of SPSS again acknowledged this approach of using the program; in Version 17, the syntax facility has been restyled and made more user friendly.

How to Use SPSS Syntax presents an overview of common SPSS commands and contains a collection of more or less independent sections where one can find specific information. All syntax in this book can be run by *any* version of SPSS.

We have assumed that the reader has some basic knowledge of SPSS, which can be obtained from any introductory SPSS textbook. For didactical reasons, we use clear-cut examples from real scientific research, while the reader is invited to replicate the findings. We have also included the relevant outcomes for reference. All data and syntax, and a lot more, can be found on the Internet pages (see http://www.ru.nl/mt/syntax/home) that go with this textbook.

Manfred te Grotenhuis
Chris Visscher
Radboud University Nijmegen, The Netherlands

Acknowledgments

I wish to thank my mentor Theo van der Weegen, who never grew tired of pointing out the relevance of SPSS syntax in social science research. When I first entered Radboud University as a student in 1990, I was amazed at his SPSS programming skills. In fact, they still seem magical to me. Many times I have thought that we had finally stumbled on the limits of SPSS syntax, but he never failed to stretch them even further. The SPSS commands presented in this book are only a (very useful) glimpse of his "magic." Luckily, we are able to show some more of it on the Internet pages that go with this textbook. I would also like to thank Hans Schmeets and Peer Scheepers for inviting me to write an English version of my Dutch textbook on SPSS syntax. It surely helped pave the way to this international edition. To write books, you must be half crazy at the very least; thanks to Anita for letting me be so from time to time.

—*Manfred te Grotenhuis*

Way back in the 1980s, the head of the department of methodology, Professor Bert Felling, asked me to write a student's guide to SPSS syntax. The seeds for this were already planted in 1981 by my colleagues Theo van der Weegen and the late Jacques van der Putten. I am sure they would be proud to see their initial ideas published with SAGE more than three decades later.

—*Chris Visscher*

We both wish to express our gratitude to Rob Eisinga, Bert Felling, Nan Dirk de Graaf, Ariana Need, and Peer Scheepers for providing all the relevant statistical data collected in the Netherlands from 1979 to 2005. Marijn Scholte greatly helped in translating the original Dutch textbook *SPSS met Syntax*. Special thanks to Matthew "Iron Man" Bennett for correcting our initial manuscripts and for providing indispensable advice on English usage. We extend our special thanks to Marijn Haverbeke and all other students from Radboud University Nijmegen, the Netherlands, whom we had the privilege to meet and who contributed to the improvement of our SPSS syntax lecture materials over the past 25 years. We thank the people at IBM SPSS for kindly allowing us to use the screenshots of their program. Last but not least, we are most grateful to the staff at SAGE Publications, in particular Vicki Knight, who immediately got enthusiastic about the project and made us feel at home within a day, and her editorial assistant, Jessica Miller.

The authors and SAGE Publications also acknowledge the following reviewers for their contributions to this text:

James R. Anthos, *South University, Columbia, SC*

Paul Ankomah, *North Carolina A&T State University*

George W. Burruss, *Southern Illinois University Carbondale*

Robert M. Clark, *Pennsylvania Highlands Community College*

Michael Duggan, *Suffolk University*

Victor Ferreros, *Walden University*

Jonathan Varhola, *Wright State University*

1

SPSS Syntax Usage

1.1 Introduction △

SPSS[1] is a user-friendly program because most options can be found in clear menus. More experienced users will, however, use syntax files, in which commands are stored to modify and/or to analyze the data. Syntax files keep track of every modification and analysis, making it possible to control and to replicate scientific results—two necessary conditions for scientific research. This book provides an overview of the most commonly used commands in terms of SPSS syntax. It is by no means meant to be a complete overview. For specialized applications, we refer to the very extensive manual, which is included in the program as a PDF file (see the help menu) for the exact notation of the commands. Moreover, a set of examples for specialized commands can be found on the Internet pages that support this book (see http://www.ru.nl/mt/syntax/home).

When using SPSS syntax, you will find that there are often several ways to achieve the same results. In such cases, we have striven to explain the least complicated method.

Some familiarity with modifying and analyzing statistical data is required from the reader as this book only deals with the practical use of SPSS syntax and not the underlying statistical techniques. For an approachable introduction to these techniques that does not require prior knowledge of mathematics, we refer the reader to *Discovering Statistics Using SPSS* (2012) by Andy Field.

How to Use SPSS Syntax is set up as a collection of independent sections where information can be found on specific commands. So it is possible to skip parts of the book that deal with topics that one is not familiar with or that are not needed. Where extra knowledge is required for a command, we will refer to the relevant section(s) of the book. However, when describing the commands, we assume that the reader has read Chapter 2 of this book in which general rules for preparing syntax are described, before reading (sections from) Chapters 3 or 4. In the following sections, we will provide some general information about how to use this book.

---

[1]SPSS is now IBM SPSS. SPSS was acquired by IBM in October 2009.

△ 1.2 Structure of the Book

To help the reader learn SPSS syntax, we have included a variety of examples from research in the social sciences. These examples are stored in SPSS data files (we use the "sav" format) and are freely available online (see http://www.ru.nl/mt/syntax/home). When downloading these files, it is recommended to store them in a directory named DATA. You may alter this destination directory, but the syntax used in this book refers to the directory DATA. It is assumed that this directory is created on the c-drive when using a Windows computer (*notation*: c:\data). This eventually means that you have to alter this reference in the syntax accordingly when you use a directory other than c:\data. We further programmed the results to be stored in c:\data as well, but again, you may adapt this to your own needs. In case the reader has a Macintosh computer, all notations in this book referring to computer files are without c:, so only \data.

The syntax used throughout this book is placed in a "box" to separate it from normal text so that it can be easily located. The syntax is then summarized again at the end of each chapter. The reader is invited to type the syntax from the book into syntax files to maximize the benefits of learning by doing. As a final reference for the reader, we have also included the relevant outcomes of analyses.

In SPSS, it is also possible to copy the commands from the menus into syntax files (this is called "pasting") and adapt them to one's needs. This is particularly useful for statistical analyses. In Chapter 4, we will elaborate this approach of creating syntax files.

From Chapter 3 onward, the book consists of more or less independent sections. In each section, one common SPSS command is explained by naming its function and the exact structure, followed by one or more examples and the most relevant results that originate from that particular command.

△ 1.3 What Is SPSS Syntax?

Up until the 1990s, SPSS did not have any menus or windows. To modify and analyze data, one would write a "job"—a series of commands—and then have SPSS execute these commands. Over the years, software has become more accessible, and SPSS added a graphical user interface with (usually) clear menus. The program, however, is still constructed in the same way. So behind all menus still lie the commands that originally had to be typed manually. These commands become visible again when pushing the "paste" button in the menus. These SPSS commands are nothing but text in which the name of the command is entered, followed by the options. Furthermore, in most commands, you will find one or more variables to which the command refers. These commands exist for almost all functions of SPSS, and all data modifications and analyses are made up of a series of commands. Managing SPSS using syntax is still a very viable way of working. The reasons for this are explained in the next section.

1.4 The Usefulness of SPSS Syntax △

Saving all actions in a syntax file has its advantages when modifying and analyzing data. In such a file, you can check exactly which commands have been executed and repair any mistakes if something went wrong. For example, when you have recoded a variable and made a mistake, it is possible that all the executed analyses since are also incorrect. Repairing the error and executing all actions again is relatively easy in a syntax file. This, of course, is much more efficient than starting again from scratch. Another advantage is that commands from a syntax file can be copied directly into a new syntax file. By changing only the variable names in the syntax, you can avoid having to find out how the modifications and analyses are done in SPSS again and again. Last, working with syntax files has the advantage that even others can read and know exactly what has been done with respect to data modifications and statistical analyses. The advantages are so great that not only experienced SPSS users but also beginners (e.g., students who are working on a paper or thesis) often work with syntax. As mentioned earlier, SPSS syntax can be created by the "paste" button in almost all SPSS menus. As this book will prove, however, you can, besides being flexible, work faster and more efficiently when typing the syntax directly into a syntax file. Additionally, not all of the features within SPSS are included in the menus.

1.5 Syntax Window △

Besides the data and output windows, SPSS also has a syntax window to type the syntax lines. The largest part of this window contains space for writing text (commands). The window also has a lot of the menus that are present in the other windows. An empty syntax window is opened by choosing File → New → Syntax. To open an existing syntax file, choose File → Open → Syntax. An important menu in the syntax window is Run, which is used to execute the commands in the syntax window. To run selected commands fast, use the *Crtl-r* shortcut (press the control button and "r" at the same time). If nothing is selected in the window, SPSS will execute the part of the syntax where the cursor is positioned. There are different ways to select syntax: If you want to execute a selection of all the commands, you can select the commands you want by "dragging" the mouse (holding the left mouse button and moving the mouse) or by holding the shift button and moving the cursor with the arrow keys. Selecting all commands can be done using the *Crtl-a* shortcut.

As explained earlier, you can also use the "paste" button in the SPSS menus. This will paste the selected commands in the menu into the syntax window that is active. This command can then be executed using the *Ctrl-r* shortcut or by the *Run* option in the menu.

Finally, we want to point out that SPSS does not have an option to automatically save syntax, so if the computer crashes, you will lose the syntax! However, it is possible to recover your syntax if it was saved in the session journal. To check this, go to the menu and select Edit → Options (SPSS Version 15 and earlier) or Edit → Options → File Locations, and then check "Record syntax in Journal" and "Append," and click on ok. We recommend saving the syntax files regularly, especially before (blocks of) commands are executed. You can save quickly by using the *Ctrl-s* shortcut.

△ 1.6 SPSS Syntax Files: An Example

Open the SPSS program to begin your session. Do not open any data yet—it does not matter if the data window is empty. Open a new syntax window with File → New → Syntax. In most cases, a data file must be opened first. To do this, type the following command into the syntax file (please note that the period (.) at the end of the command is part of the syntax):

> GET FILE "c:/data/chapter1.sav".
>
> * *Macintosh computers use:* GET FILE "/data/chapter1.sav".

In this command, it is assumed that the file "chapter1.sav" is located in c:/data/. If necessary, replace this with the directory where you have saved it on your own computer. Instead of the double straight quotation marks before and after the file name in SPSS syntax, one may also use straight single quotes, *but* back quotes (`) are not allowed. Furthermore, please note the period (.) after the command. If everything seems in order, execute the command by placing the cursor on the command line and pushing *Ctrl-r* or choosing Run → Current from the menu. If you did not make any mistakes, the data window should now show the data from the example file. If this is not the case, there will be an error message in the output window indicating the error made in the syntax command. After loading the data into SPSS, you may retrieve specific information from it. To obtain information about the variables, please type the following command after the GET FILE command and execute the command:

> DISPLAY DICTIONARY.

A description of all variables will appear in the output window after executing this command (Table 1.1):

Table 1.1 The Results of Display Dictionary

		Variable Information			
Variable	Label	Measurement Level	Column Width	Alignment	Print Format
respnr	Respondent identification number	Nominal	8	Right	F5
SEX	<None>	Nominal	8	Right	F1
EDUC	Highest completed educational level	Ordinal	8	Right	F1
YBIRTH	Year respondent was born	Scale	8	Right	F4

Note: Variables in the working file.

Variable Values		
Value		Label
SEX	1	Male
	2	Female
EDUC	1	Elementary school
	2	Middle school
	3	Junior high school
	4	Senior high school
	5	Vocational school
	6	College
	7	Bachelor degrees
	8	Master degrees

Apparently, a variable called YBIRTH is present in the data file containing the year of birth of the respondents. The data in the file "chapter1.sav" were collected in 1995, so we are able to calculate the respondent's age with the formula "1995 – YBIRTH." The syntax is as follows (please type it in your syntax file and run it):

```
COMPUTE AGE = 1995 – YBIRTH.
```

You have now created a variable AGE containing the age of each respondent in the file. If you want to check whether the new variable is correctly computed, you can execute the following command:

```
DESCRIPTIVES AGE YBIRTH

/STATISTICS MEAN STDDEV MIN MAX.
```

This will produce an output that displays the mean, standard deviation, and minimum and maximum values of AGE and YBIRTH. After executing the syntax, the following will be displayed in the output window (Table 1.2):

Table 1.2 Descriptive Statistics of AGE and YBIRTH

Descriptive Statistics					
	N	**Minimum**	**Maximum**	**Mean**	**Std. Deviation**
AGE	1974	18.00	70.00	42.2533	13.74781
YBIRTH year respondent was born	1974	1925	1977	1952.75	13.748
Valid N (listwise)	1974				

The computation of AGE is correct, since the minimum value for YBIRTH is 1925 and the maximum value for AGE is 70 (1995–1925). Furthermore, the number of valid scores is equal for both variables (1974). Finally, the sum of the two mean scores is equal to 1995 (42.2533 + 1952.7467).

Another variable present in the data file is SEX. A frequency distribution is useful to get full information about this variable (Table 1.3):

```
FREQUENCIES SEX.
```

Table 1.3 Frequency Distribution of SEX

		SEX			
		Frequency	**Percent**	**Valid Percent**	**Cumulative Percent**
Valid	1 Male	945	47.9	47.9	47.9
	2 Female	1029	52.1	52.1	100.0
	Total	1974	100.0	100.0	

This provides us with a table including the absolute numbers and percentage of men and women in the data file.

As you may have noticed, the data operations and descriptions in this chapter have been executed with relatively simple commands. The next chapter deals with the general structure of such commands. In Chapters 3 and 4, the individual commands are described in more detail.

1.7 SPSS Syntax: An Overview △

We conclude by listing all of the syntax used in this chapter. Notice that syntax comments can be made by starting a sentence with an asterisk (*) and ending it with a period (.). This is a useful way to annotate your work for future reference. The syntax (Windows and Macintosh) is also available at the website (http://www.ru.nl/mt/syntax/home).

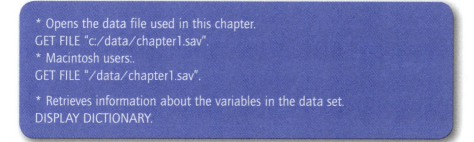

```
* Opens the data file used in this chapter.
GET FILE "c:/data/chapter1.sav".
* Macintosh users:.
GET FILE "/data/chapter1.sav".

* Retrieves information about the variables in the data set.
DISPLAY DICTIONARY.
```

```
* Creates a new variable AGE (sample is from 1995).
COMPUTE AGE = 1995 − YBIRTH.

* Checks whether new variable was computed correctly.
DESCRIPTIVES AGE YBIRTH
 /STATISTICS MEAN STDDEV MIN MAX.

* Shows the frequency distribution of the variable SEX.
FREQUENCIES SEX.
```

Basic Knowledge

As mentioned in the introduction (Chapter 1), all SPSS commands begin with the name of the data operation or statistical analysis you want to execute. For example, the command to open a file begins with GET. Likewise, to obtain the frequency distribution, you start the command with FREQUENCIES. The name of the data operation is usually abbreviated to the first three letters: FRE will get you the same result in SPSS as FREQUENCIES. This also explains why spelling errors often go unnoticed: FREQUENSEIS will be "read" as FRE (QUENCIES). Usage of too many abbreviations or personal spelling is, however, not recommended because it will make the syntax difficult for others to read. After the name of the command, it is possible to add a number of subcommands and you will always have to end the command with a period. This period sign (.) has to be at the end of the line so that SPSS can distinguish between the sign that ends the command and a period sign that is used as a separator in a number with decimals. The subcommands are used to further specify what needs to be done. They are used, for instance, to indicate which variables the command refers to, what results to display, and what statistical method to use.

All possible subcommands will be specified in the detailed descriptions in Chapters 3 and 4. These subcommands are separated by a forward slash (/). The readability of the syntax is improved if every subcommand is placed on a new line and indented by a few spaces so that it is clear that they go with the main command. For example,

```
GET FILE "c:/data/chapter2.sav".
* Macintosh users:.
GET FILE "/data/chapter2.sav".

FREQUENCIES
 /VARIABLES EDUC
 /FORMAT DVALUE
 /STATISTICS MEAN MEDIAN.
```

In this syntax, the file "chapter2.sav" is opened, and subsequently a frequency distribution is requested for the variable EDUC (educational level). The line "/FORMAT DVALUE" indicates that the values should be displayed in descending order. If you do not add this subcommand, the values are presented in ascending order. The last line of the syntax indicates that the mean and median of education should be displayed. Note that only the last line ends with a period. If you had placed the period sign after the first subcommand, the command would end after the command FREQUENCIES for education. The result of this would be that the values are presented in ascending order, and the mean and median are not displayed (meaning that all subcommands after the period sign are not executed). Table 2.1 displays the results of the full command.

Table 2.1 Mean, Median, and Frequency Distribution of EDUC

Statistics		
EDUC		
N	Valid	1974
	Missing	0
Mean		4.31
Median		4.00

EDUC		Frequency	Percent	Valid Percent	Cumulative Percent
Valid	8 Master degree	144	7.3	7.3	7.3
	7 Bachelor degree	388	19.7	19.7	27.0
	6 College	140	7.1	7.1	34.0
	5 Vocational school	133	6.7	6.7	40.8
	4 Senior high school	393	19.9	19.9	60.7
	3 Junior high school	220	11.1	11.1	71.8
	2 Middle school	339	17.2	17.2	89.0
	1 Elementary school	217	11.0	11.0	100.0
	Total	1974	100.0	100.0	

The sequence of the subcommands is fixed for most commands. When specifying multiple subcommands, it is therefore necessary to maintain the order in which they are presented in this book. You can use either small or capital letters when you are entering commands in the syntax window, as SPSS deals with them in the same way. So it does not matter if you type "Frequencies," "FREQUENCIES," or "FrEqUeNcIeS." However, try to be consistent in your style, so that the syntax will remain clear.

Anywhere a space is used in the syntax, you are allowed to use a comma, return, tab, or multiple spaces. You can, for instance, use this in a long list of variables to divide them over a number of lines. Again, it makes sense to indent a few spaces to show that these lines go with the main command. There should not be an empty line in a command (by two consecutive returns or a blank line with only spaces or tabs), because this will result in partial execution of a command or no execution at all.

2.2 Variable Names and Variable Lists △

Until SPSS Version 11 only 8 characters were allowed for a variable name. This required some creativity to devise logical names, but the syntax is easier to understand when the meaning of the variable is clear. This problem is solved from Version 12 onward because the variable name can have up to 64 characters. It is recommended, however, not to use names that are too long, because this will decrease the efficiency of using SPSS syntax in the first place. Variable names should always begin with a letter and not with a numeral, such as "3rdmeasurement." However, you can use numbers in other places within the variable. Likewise, you cannot use spaces and the symbols "," ";" ":" "()" and "@" in variable names. The symbol "_" (underscore) can be used instead of a space (for instance, var_1). Furthermore, the names are not case sensitive, so SPSS does not distinguish between small letters and capital letters (var_1 and VAR_1 relate to the same variable).

To improve the clarity of the output, you can assign a label to the variable, which can be as long as 255 characters and may also contain spaces. See the command VARIABLE LABELS (p. 26) for an explanation of variable labeling.

A common subcommand is the variable list. In the example in Section 2.1, only one variable was specified in the subcommand "/VARIABLES." However, it's almost always possible to specify more than one variable at the same time. A command like FREQUENCIES will then give a separate frequency distribution for each variable. If a command refers to the relationship between variables, like CORRELATIONS, the whole set of specified variables is used in one analysis. Specifying multiple variables is done by putting them in sequence, separated by spaces. For efficiency, one may use the word "TO" between two variables. SPSS will then include all variables that are listed in the data set in between these two specified variables. This is especially useful when dealing with scale constructions, which usually consist of a series of variables. Please note that when using TO, the variable that is the most left in the data window is specified first; otherwise it will not work. The word "ALL" can also be used when you want to use all variables in the data file. It is clear from the above that a number of variable names are not allowed in SPSS because they have a specific meaning. The following are prohibited: ALL, TO, AND, OR, NOT, BY, WITH, EQ, NE, LT, LE, GT, and GE.

△ 2.3 **Strings**

A string consists of a row of characters (letters, numbers, or punctuation). Often, a string is no more than a piece of text. Strings are common in SPSS commands, for example, the name of the data file you want to open or the label of a variable. Strings are not the same as so-called identifiers, like command names or variable names, which also consist of a number of characters. *Identifiers* have a distinct meaning in SPSS, while a string is just treated as a neutral piece of text. To distinguish between identifiers and strings, and to keep a string with spaces and punctuation together, the strings should always be put between either single or double quotation marks. For instance, in the case of the extended variable name (label) of the variable EDUC,

VARIABLE LABELS EDUC

"Educational level of respondent".

You may execute the command FREQUENCIES from Section 2.1 again to check whether this command was properly executed (for results, see Table 2.2).

Table 2.2 EDUC With Label "Educational Level of Respondent"

Statistics		
EDUC: Educational Level of Respondent		
N	Valid	1974
	Missing	0
Mean		4.31
Median		4.00

Note: In case the label is not shown, please change the table labeling to "Names and Labels" in Edit → Options . . . → Output labels → Pivot Table Labeling

2.4 Arithmetic Expressions △

Arithmetic expressions consist of calculations. In our earlier expression "1995 – YBIRTH" (p. 6), the age of the respondents was calculated. A typical example of a command that requires an arithmetic expression is COMPUTE (p. 34), which creates a new variable.

The symbols used are self-explanatory for the most part: "+" to add, "–" to subtract, "*" to multiply, "/" to divide, and "**" for exponentiation. SPSS applies the standard rules for the sequence of operations (multiplication comes before addition, etc.), but when in doubt, it is better to use parentheses to separate pieces of the calculation. For example, "AGE – 18/10" means that age is reduced by 1.8, while "(AGE – 18)/10" means that age first is reduced by 18, and the result is then divided by 10. Besides this, SPSS can do a lot of other calculations within expressions, for example, calculating the square root or mean. For detailed information, we refer you to the appendix on arithmetic expressions (p. 117).

2.5 Logical Expressions △

A logical expression resembles an arithmetic expression. However, a logical expression holds a statement that can only be true or false. Therefore, the result of this sort of calculation is either "true" or "false." For example, the logical expression "AGE > 18" is true for all respondents aged 19 years or older, and false for the rest. Certain commands require a logical expression such as SELECT IF, which excludes all respondents who do not meet a specific condition from an analysis. For example, we will select respondents younger than 25 years of age:

SELECT IF AGE < 25.

To check the execution of this command, type the command FREQUENCIES from Section 2.1 again, but with AGE instead of EDUC (for results, see Table 2.3).

Table 2.3 Frequency Distribution of AGE After Selection (<Age 25)

AGE Respondent's Age				
	Frequency	**Percent**	**Valid Percent**	**Cumulative Percent**
24.00	46	22.3	22.3	22.3
23.00	31	15.0	15.0	37.4
22.00	31	15.0	15.0	52.4
21.00	36	17.5	17.5	69.9
20.00	14	6.8	6.8	76.7
19.00	35	17.0	17.0	93.7
18.00	13	6.3	6.3	100.0
Total	206	100.0	100.0	

Variable names and numbers are often used in logical expressions with symbols in between to indicate the relationship. Most of you will be familiar with these symbols: ">" means greater than, "<" means lesser than, and "=" means equal to. You can combine these expressions to form ">=", greater than or equal to; "<=", lesser than or equal to; and "<>", unequal to (the order of the symbols is fixed, so you cannot use "=>"). You can use either two variables in a logical expression (to compare the age of the respondent with that of his or her partner, e.g., "AGE > AGEPART") or a variable in combination with a number ("AGE > 18"). You can expand the expressions mentioned above by adding logical operations to them. The simple logical operations are AND, OR, and NOT. The command "SELECT IF (AGE > 18) AND (AGE < 40)" simply means that all respondents between 19 and 39 years of age are selected. The command "SELECT IF NOT (AGE = 23)" means that respondents aged 23 years will be excluded. It is wise to use parentheses for more elaborate expressions so that it is clear not only to the reader but also for the SPSS program that runs it. Additional information on logical expressions can be found in the appendix (p. 121).

2.6 Comments △

In SPSS, it is possible to include text in a syntax file that is inactive. The lines below do not execute anything when you run them:

> * The asterisk before the two lines
>
> prevents it from performing any function.

By incorporating text that is not intended to modify or analyze data, it is possible to add extra information to the syntax file, which is why these texts are called comments. A comment starts with an asterisk (*) and ends with a period. The comment can be just one line of text, but as seen in the example above, the text can also be of several lines in length. Please bear in mind that within the comment there cannot be any period signs, because this will terminate the comment, and SPSS will try to execute the rest as a command. It is also possible to (temporarily) switch off a command by placing an asterisk before it.

Because the syntax itself is usually somewhat cryptic, it makes sense to use comments to clarify the most important parts of the syntax file. You can start, for instance, with a brief description of the function of the file. Furthermore, for each command or group of commands, you can describe their function and possible results of the analyses, so that the syntax file can be read as text. The comments can also serve as a reminder when you need to use the syntax again later. When sharing the syntax with others, it almost goes without saying that comprehensively clarifying comments are added to the syntax.

We also recommend deleting superfluous commands so that the syntax file remains compact and clear with data operations and analyses. A good final syntax file should be executable as a whole, that is, without first having to execute certain selections. However, it is also true that you might be confronted with bad syntax files where the appropriate commands are still interspersed with various bits of experimental commands. To obtain the desired results, pieces of syntax must be executed selectively, which may be a hazardous enterprise. So we recommend turning your final syntax file into a clear-cut piece of syntax (art) without any errors or unnecessary commands. When stored this way, you have developed a powerful analytical tool that can be shared with others and allows for replication and control.

△ 2.7 The Explanation of SPSS Syntax Commands

The following chapters will focus in detail on various SPSS syntax commands. Every command will be explained in a separate section, which will start with a brief overview of the command—what each command is used for, and why it is needed for research. We then describe the structure of the command, followed by an example and the results. Additionally, sometimes we describe some of the optional subcommands and their results when needed.

All commands described in this book can also be found in the PDF file SPSSbase.pdf. You can request this *Command Syntax Reference* via the help function in SPSS (see Figure 2.1). The explanations in that PDF file are comprehensive, but can, at times, be cryptic and technical in places. A second alternative way to quickly see what a command should look like is to type the first three letters of the command in a syntax file. You then have to select these letters with the mouse and click on the "syntax help" option on the toolbar (see Figure 2.1 where fre [frequencies] is selected).

Figure 2.1 Syntax Help Function

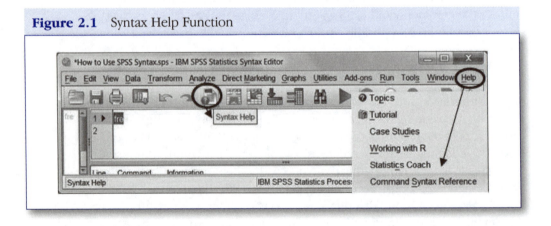

The extensive help function in SPSS will open in a new window, with the full syntax that goes with the selected command. Further information about the command, and about the syntax in general, can be found in the left-hand column (see Figure 2.2). A third, previously mentioned, option is to use the menus to compose the whole command and then paste and adjust it manually (see Figures 2.3a–c).

Figure 2.2 Syntax Help Function After Selecting fre in the Syntax File and Clicking on the "Syntax Help" Button (See Figure 2.1)

```
FREQUENCIES VARIABLES=varlist [varlist...]

[/FORMAT= [{NOTABLE }]  [{AVALUE**}]
           {LIMIT(n)}    {DVALUE  }
                         {AFREQ   }
                         {DFREQ   }


[/MISSING=INCLUDE]

[/BARCHART=[MINIMUM(n)] [MAXIMUM(n)] [{FREQ(n)    }]]
                                     {PERCENT(n) }

[/PIECHART=[MINIMUM(n)] [MAXIMUM(n)] [{FREQ    }] [{MISSING  }]]
                                     {PERCENT}    {NOMISSING}

[/HISTOGRAM=[MINIMUM(n)]  [MAXIMUM(n)] [{FREQ(n)   }] [{NONORMAL}] ]
                                                      {NORMAL  }

[/GROUPED=varlist [{(width)         }]]
                  {(boundary list)}

[/NTILES=n]

[/PERCENTILES=value list]

[/STATISTICS=[DEFAULT] [MEAN] [STDDEV] [MINIMUM] [MAXIMUM]
             [SEMEAN] [VARIANCE] [SKEWNESS] [SESKEW] [RANGE]
             [MODE] [KURTOSIS] [SEKURT] [MEDIAN] [SUM] [ALL]
               [NONE]]

[/ORDER=[{ANALYSIS}] [{VARIABLE}]
```

Figure 2.3a Retrieving Frequency Distributions Using the Menu

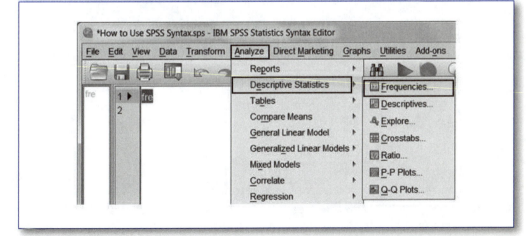

Figure 2.3b Menu and Submenus That Will Appear After Selecting Frequencies (See Figure 2.3a)

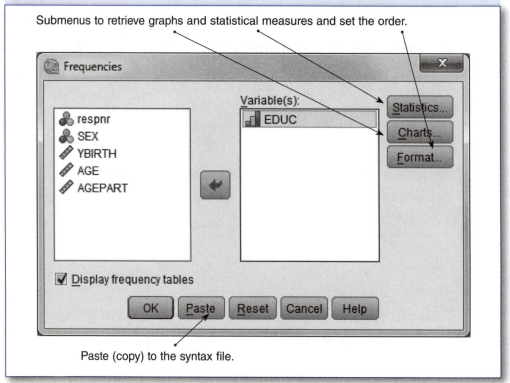

Figure 2.3c The Result of "Paste" (See Figure 2.3b)

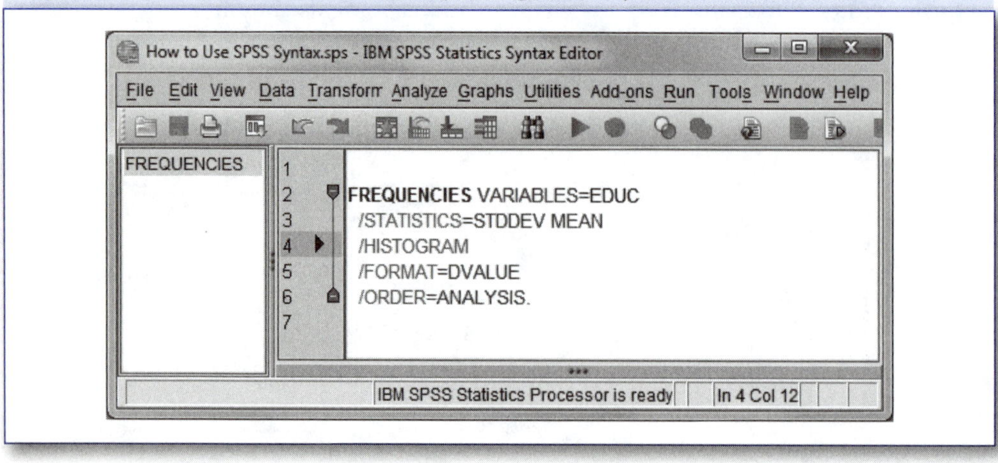

Note: Subcommands include the standard deviation, mean, and a histogram, while the values in the frequency table are to be presented in descending order.

2.8 SPSS Syntax: An Overview △

In conclusion, the syntax used in this chapter is listed below.

```
* Opens the data file used in this chapter.
GET FILE "c:/data/chapter2.sav".
* Macintosh users:.
GET FILE "/data/chapter2.sav".

* Shows frequency distributions of education and median and mean.
FREQUENCIES
 /VARIABLES EDUC
 /FORMAT DVALUE
 /STATISTICS MEAN MEDIAN.

* Adds description to variable education.
VARIABLE LABELS EDUC
 "Educational level respondent".

* Checks education for variable label.
FREQUENCIES
 /VARIABLES EDUC
 /FORMAT DVALUE
 /STATISTICS MEAN MEDIAN.

* Selects respondents younger than 25.
SELECT IF AGE < 25.

* Checks whether selection on age was done correctly.
 FREQUENCIES
 /VARIABLES AGE
 /FORMAT DVALUE
 /STATISTICS MEAN MEDIAN.
```

3

Data Modifications

3.1 Introduction △

This chapter deals with commands for modifying data files. Most of these commands are common applications and are widely used in research. They will be addressed here under 26 different sections. This way, more experienced users can find specific commands quickly and easily. For readers who are not familiar with the commands, it is recommended to read the entire chapter to appreciate the full potential of SPSS and working with syntax. The commands that are discussed here are summarized at the end of the chapter. For those who want to reproduce the results in any section, please always execute the command in Section 3.2 that opens the data set together with the commands that are listed under **example** and/or **results** in the particular section(s).

3.2 GET △

Function

The GET command is used to open an SPSS data file with the extension *.sav*. In general, this will be the first command in a syntax file. It is also possible to exclude a number of variables within this command or to rename variables.

Structure

The GET command is followed by the FILE subcommand and is specified as a string, specifying the directory (c:\data); for Macintosh computers, it is only \data and the name of the data file (chapter3.sav) (Figure 3.1).

Example

```
GET FILE "c:/data/chapter3.sav".
* Macintosh users:.
GET FILE "/data/chapter3.sav".
```

Results

Figure 3.1 The File "chapter3.sav" Is Opened With GET

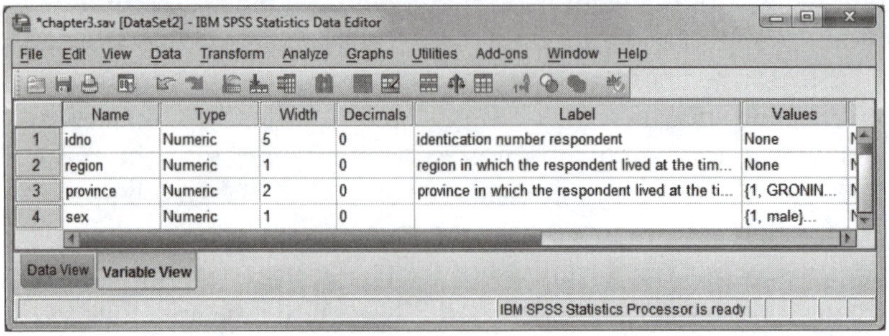

Optional Subcommands

The KEEP subcommand allows you to specify the variables that you want to include in the file that is to be opened. You must list these variables directly (after a space) after KEEP. The remaining variables in the data file that are not listed are removed from future analyses. If this subcommand is omitted, all variables from the file are included.

Similarly, the DROP subcommand ignores the specified variables and includes those not listed instead.

The RENAME command is, unsurprisingly, used to rename variables. This command is followed by the name of an existing variable, an equal sign (=), and the new variable name. If more variables need renaming, you can then leave a space and specify the next variable that needs to be renamed.

Extensive Example

```
GET FILE "c:/data/chapter3.sav"
/DROP LIST FUTURE
/RENAME GOD2 = BELIEVE_NOW GOD1 = BELIEVE_15.
EXECUTE.
```

This command opens the "chapter3.sav" file. The variables LIST and FUTURE are removed, and the variables GOD1 and GOD2 are given more meaningful names (i.e., BELIEVE_NOW and BELIEVE_15; note the use of underscores) (Figure 3.2). Finally, the syntax ends with the EXECUTE command. When using the KEEP and DROP subcommands, some versions of SPSS display the information in the data window only *after* the EXECUTE command is executed, which can be irritating for some users. See Section 3.4 for more information (p. 26).

Results

Figure 3.2   Variables "God1" and "God2" Renamed and LIST/FUTURE Omitted

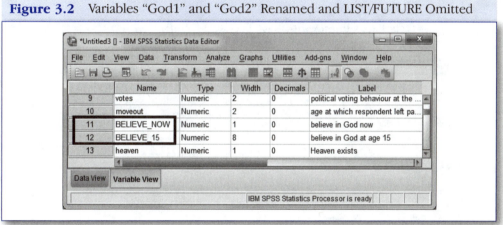

3.3 SAVE △

Function

The SAVE command saves the data file. This is used after recoding variables, constructing scales, or other data operations. It is advisable not to overwrite the original data file (see Figure 3.3 on page 24). As mistakes are bound to occur, it is better to keep the original file as a backup—so rename the file you want to save. SAVE can also be used to save a file that contains only relevant variables from the current file. This makes the data set easier for others to use, and it also reduces the size (in bytes) of the file, which makes it easier for direct e-mailing. We like to add that there are free transfer programs available on the Internet (up to 2 GB or more) in case the .sav file is still too large.

Structure

The SAVE command is always followed by the OUTFILE subcommand, which in turn is followed by the directory and file name as a string.

Example

```
SAVE OUTFILE "c:/data/chapter3new.sav".
```

Results

```
GET FILE "c:/data/chapter3new.sav".
```

Figure 3.3   The File "chapter3new.sav" Is Opened With GET

Optional Subcommands

As with the GET command, the KEEP subcommand can be added to save a limited number of variables. The KEEP subcommand should be followed by a list of variables that you wish to save.

As mentioned, the DROP subcommand is the counterpart of KEEP: The variables specified here will *not* be saved. This subcommand is used if you want to omit a number of variables through the syntax. Just open the file with the GET command and save it with the redundant variables specified with DROP.

The RENAME command can be used to save variables under a different name. The name of an existing variable, an equal sign (=), and the new variable name follows this RENAME command. If you need to rename more variables, you can leave a space and specify the next variable that needs to be renamed.

Extensive Example

```
SAVE OUTFILE "c:/data/chapter3short.sav"
/KEEP IDNO SEX EDUC YBIRTH VOTES
/RENAME VOTES = POLITICS.
```

Following this command, five variables are saved from the old file into the new file "chapter3short.sav," and the variable VOTES is now renamed as POLITICS (Figure 3.4).

Results

```
GET FILE "c:/data/chapter3short.sav".
```

Figure 3.4 The File "chapter3short.sav" Opened With GET

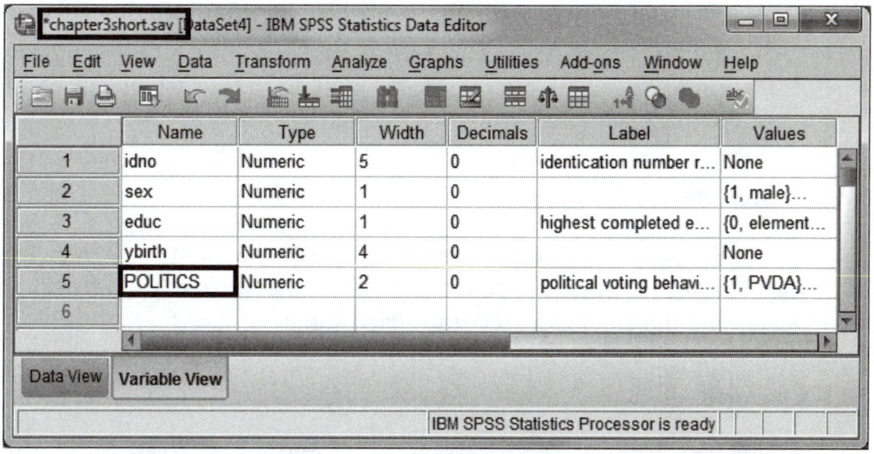

Note: If you want to proceed to the next section, the file "chapter3.sav" has to be reopened (so execute the GET command from Section 3.2 again).

△ 3.4 EXECUTE

Function

It is more efficient for SPSS to postpone some data transformations until they are actually required. As discussed in the GET command example, some versions of SPSS only display the data in the data window *after* you run the EXECUTE command. However, when a statistical procedure is run—such as FREQUENCIES—SPSS will run an (invisible) EXECUTE command instead. So if you use the EXECUTE command, it will release all SPSS operations that are still queued.

Structure

EXECUTE does not have any subcommands, so you can just use the command together with a period (.) to end the command.

Example

```
EXECUTE.
```

△ 3.5 VARIABLE LABELS

Function

VARIABLE LABELS allows you to make detailed descriptions ("labels") for each variable. These labels will appear in the output window, making the results more readable. It is therefore possible to clarify ambiguous variable names with a clear label using this command.

Structure

The VARIABLE LABELS command (please note that commands can have two words) is followed by the name(s) of one or more variables. A string variable containing the label is placed after each variable.

Example

```
VARIABLE LABELS
LEAVECHURCH "age at which the respondent left the church"
YBIRTH "year of birth of the respondent".
```

To see if the variable labels were applied properly, you may run a frequency table of the variables (Table 3.1):

Results

```
FREQUENCIES
 /VARIABLES LEAVECHURCH YBIRTH.
```

Table 3.1 Variable Labels for LEAVECHURCH and YBIRTH

Statistics			
		leavechurch age at which the respondent left the church	**ybirth year of birth of the respondent**
N	Valid	1974	1974
	Missing	0	0

3.6 VALUE LABELS △

Function

The VALUE LABELS command is similar to the VARIABLE LABELS command in that it also assigns a label. With this command, however, the label is not assigned to a variable but to the categories of that variable. This is especially useful for variables with a nominal or ordinal measurement level, where the meaning of the categories cannot be deduced from the numbers of the categories. The categories are named in such a way that their meaning is clear from reading the results in the output file.

Structure

The VALUE LABELS command is followed by the name of one or more variables. A list follows this command with a value and the label for that value in quotes. After a slash, more variables can be specified with the values and labels.

Example

```
VALUE LABELS SEX 1 "Male" 2 "Female"
 /REGION 1 "North" 2 "East" 3 "West" 4 "South".
```

To see if the value labels were applied properly, you may run a frequency table of the two variables (Table 3.2):

Results

```
FREQUENCIES
    /VARIABLES SEX REGION.
```

Table 3.2 Value Labels of SEX and REGION

Sex		Frequency	Percent	Valid Percent	Cumulative Percent
Valid	1 Male	945	47.9	47.9	47.9
	2 Female	1029	52.1	52.1	100.0
	Total	1974	100.0	100.0	

Region where the respondent was interviewed		Frequency	Percent	Valid Percent	Cumulative Percent
Valid	1 North	217	11.0	11.0	11.0
	2 East	441	22.3	22.3	33.3
	3 West	891	45.1	45.1	78.5
	4 South	425	21.5	21.5	100.0
	Total	1974	100.0	100.0	

△ 3.7 MISSING VALUES

Function

The units of analysis (often respondents) can have missing (unfilled) scores on variables and/or invalid scores (scores that may not be useful in the analysis). In SPSS, missing scores (i.e., no score at all) are referred to as "system missing." They occur as blanks in your data file and are automatically left out of any analysis. Invalid scores (labeled "missing values"), however, must be defined by the user. The MISSING VALUES command transforms scores into missing values (invalid scores). For example, the scores that fall into the categories "do not know" or "will not say" are often transformed into missing values first. Otherwise, SPSS will use them in analysis, which may be senseless (e.g., when calculating means).

Structure

The MISSING VALUES command is followed by the name of the variable (or multiple variables) and the values of the missing categories in parentheses. If there are several variables that share the same missing value(s), it is possible to specify the variables first and then specify the values that must be treated as invalid (see the example below). If you have many variables, instead of typing all the variable names, it is more efficient to use SPSS syntax statements like LOWEST, HIGHEST, or THRU (see Section 3.9). If you want to undo the missing values (but not the "system missings"), include parentheses without a value (i.e., (); see our example for HEAVEN in the box below).

Example

```
MISSING VALUES VOTES (14 15 16)
LEAVECHURCH CHURCHMEMBER (99).
MISSING VALUES HEAVEN ().
```

In this example, the categories/values 14, 15, and 16 ("will not say," "do not know," "does not vote") of the VOTES variable are specified as invalid, while the value 99 ("does not apply") is made invalid for the LEAVECHURCH and CHURCHMEMBER variables. Finally, all invalid values of HEAVEN are turned into valid observations (Table 3.3).

Results

```
FREQUENCIES
 /VARIABLES LEAVECHURCH CHURCHMEMBER VOTES HEAVEN.
```

Table 3.3 Missing Values for LEAVECHURCH, CHURCHMEMBER, VOTES and Validation of Initially Invalid Values for HEAVEN

		leavechurch age at which the respondent left the church	churchmember church membership	votes political voting behavior at the time of interview	heaven heaven exists
Statistics					
N	Valid	443	1966	1647	1974
	Missing	1531	8	327	0

△ 3.8 DISPLAY

Function

The DISPLAY command displays information about variables, including, among other things, variable labels to gain insights into the meaning of variables and their measurement levels, and so on.

Structure

The DISPLAY command is followed by an instruction to indicate what information is desired. DISPLAY can be followed by the VARIABLES subcommand and a list of selected variables. Leaving out this subcommand displays all available information. The LABELS command lists all variable labels, and the DICTIONARY command displays label categories, information on missing values, and the measurement levels of the variables, as well as the labels of the variables.

Example

```
DISPLAY DICTIONARY
/VARIABLES SEX MARITALSTAT EDUC.
```

Results

The output begins with a table displaying the names of the variables followed by its position in the data file (in the above example, MARITALSTAT is the 14th variable in the file). Displayed next are label, measurement level,[1] and features of the format in which the variable is stored. The line "Missing Values" indicates what values are defined as missing (see Section 3.7, p. 28). A list of values and labels follows this table. Values that are defined as missing are presented as such (Table 3.4).

Table 3.4 Information About SEX, MARTIALSTAT, and EDUC

Variable Information							
Variable	**Position**	**Label**	**Measurement Level**	**Column Width**	**Alignment**	**Print Format**	**Missing Values**
sex	4	<None>	Nominal	8	Right	F1	
maritalstat	14	Marital status	Nominal	8	Right	F1	8, 9
educ	5	Highest completed education	Ordinal	8	Right	F1	
Note: Variables in the working file.							

Variable Values		
Value		**Label**
sex	1	Male
	2	Female
maritalstat	1	Not married
	2	Married
	3	Divorced
	4	Widow
	8[a]	Won't say
	9[a]	Unknown
educ	1	Elementary school
	2	Middle school
	3	Junior high school
	4	Senior high school
	5	Vocational school
	6	College
	7	Bachelor degrees
	8	Master degrees
Note: a. Missing value.		

---

[1] The measurement level in SPSS is "scale" (=ratio/interval) by default and may be adjusted by the user if this is not correct! For the analysis and modification of data, it is not relevant which measurement level is assigned to the variable, with the exception of certain graphs and tables.

△ 3.9 RECODE

Function

RECODE is used to give variables new codes or values. For each value or set of values, a new value is specified. The new variable will usually be a nominal or an ordinal variable, while the original variable can be of any measurement level.

Structure

The RECODE command is followed by the name of the original variable. This is then followed by a value (or set of values) in parentheses, an equal sign (=), and then the new value. We recommend using INTO at the end of the command followed by a new name for the recoded variable. If this is not done, the old variable will be overwritten and the old values will be lost! This kind of recoding is thus discouraged. Please note that when using INTO the variable labels are not copied. You will have to add them yourself with the VALUE LABELS command (Section 3.6).

   To give a set of values of the original variable the same value, you can put a number of values in a row—separated by spaces—before the equal sign (=). For example, when you use (2 3 4 = 0), respondents with a value of 2, 3, or 4 will get the value 0 in the new recoded variable. You can also assign a new value to a whole interval (which is vital when recoding most interval or ratio variables) by using the command THRU. In addition, you can use the commands LOWEST and HIGHEST to indicate the lowest or highest values of the original variable. The statement "LOWEST THRU 5 = 3" means that respondents with values lesser than or equal to 5 on the original value will get a value 3 in the new variable. When recoding interval variables, it is customary to equate the upper and lower limits so that no values are missed: (0 THRU 100=1) (100 THRU 200=2). All numbers from 0 to 99.999 are recoded to 1, whereas values from 100 to 200 are recoded into 2.

   The MISSING and SYSMIS commands can be used to recode invalid or missing values. SYSMIS means that the respondent does not have a score ("a blank") on the variable ("a system missing") and is excluded from statistical analyses. MISSING indicates that the respondent does have a score, but an invalid one, and it is thus again excluded from the analysis. So "MISSING=999" and "SYSMIS=999" in a recode command mean that all missing or invalid values are recoded to the value 999.

All values that have not been recoded by the RECODE command are specified as system missing by SPSS. You can use the operator ELSE to prevent this. ELSE refers to all values that are not recoded by previous lines in the command (see the example below). There are also special cases for the value after the equal sign (=). COPY allows the variable to keep a certain old value. For example, "16 THRU HIGHEST = COPY" will leave values of 16 and higher unchanged in the new variable.

Example

```
RECODE VOTES (1 5 12 = 1) (2 4 9 10 = 2)
(3 6 THRU 8 11 = 3) (ELSE = 999) INTO POLITICS.
```

The variable VOTES is made less ambiguous with this command. The Dutch political parties are divided into left wing (1), center of politics (2), and right wing (3). All other values ("other party," "will not say," "do not know," and "does not vote") are coded (valid) value 999 (Table 3.5).

Results

```
FREQUENCIES
/VARIABLES POLITICS.
```

Table 3.5 Recoding the Variable VOTES Into a New Variable POLITICS

POLITICS				
	Frequency	**Percent**	**Valid Percent**	**Cumulative Percent**
Valid 1.00	529	26.8	26.8	26.8
2.00	609	30.9	30.9	57.6
3.00	506	25.6	25.6	83.3
999.00	330	16.7	16.7	100.0
Total	1974	100.0	100.0	

△ 3.10 COMPUTE

Function

The COMPUTE command is used to construct a variable using a formula. In Chapter 1 (Section 1.6), we used an example where age is calculated from the year of birth and the year of the interview. Another example is constructing "dummy variables"—that is, dichotomous variables with the values 0 and 1, commonly used in regression analysis (Section 4.10).

Structure

The name of the variable that is to be created follows the COMPUTE command, which is then followed by an equal sign (=) and at last the formula. If the name of the variable already exists in the data set, the old values will be replaced, but in all other cases, a new variable will be created. (An introduction on arithmetic expressions and formulas to create variables can be found on p. 13 and in the appendix on p. 117). When the command is run, the (new) variable receives the new values. These values are displayed in the data window after the EXECUTE command (see p. 26). When a variable that is included in the formula contains many "system missings" or "missing values" (see p. 28), the result of the calculation will generally be a system missing as well. This is logical because the result of "missing + 4" is unknown, so SPSS turns this into missing. This means that the new variable will have many missings when it is the product of several variables with missing or invalid values. To overcome this drawback we use MEAN (see p. 118), whereby the means are based on a fixed minimum number of variables without missing or invalid values and without taking into account missing values on the other variables.

Example

COMPUTE OWNHOME = (1995 – YBIRTH) – MOVEOUT.

MOVEOUT is a variable that indicates the age at which the respondent moved out of the parental house. The part of the formula in parentheses calculates the age of the respondent, as we have seen before. The result of the formula is the number of years that the respondent has not lived with his parents since moving. Respondents who still live with their parents will have a missing value on MOVEOUT and thus a system missing for OWN-HOME (Table 3.6).

Results

FREQUENCIES
VARIABLES OWNHOME
/STATISTICS DEFAULT.

Table 3.6   Mean, Standard Deviation, and Minimum and Maximum Value for the Variable OWNHOME

Statistics		
OWNHOME		
N	Valid	1831
	Missing	143
Mean		22.0437
Std. Deviation		12.60580
Minimum		.00
Maximum		68.00

3.11 COUNT △

Function

This command counts the number of times a certain value appears in a list of variables for each respondent. This results in a variable with a minimum value of 0 and a maximum value that equals the number of variables in the list. Generally, this command is used to count the number of missing or invalid scores a respondent has on a number of variables. It is also used to count the number of positive or negative responses that a respondent has given to a sample of questions.

Structure

The results are stored in a new variable that needs to be given a name following the COUNT command. This is followed by an equal sign (=), a blank, and then the list of variables that need values counted, and the value(s) that need counting in parentheses. If the values that need counting are not the same for every variable, it is possible to indicate a second list of variables and values. Indicating the values that need to be counted is done in the same way as indicating values in the RECODE command (for details, see p. 32). Values should be separated by spaces and the words HIGHEST, LOWEST, THRU, MISSING, and SYSMIS can be used to count the highest value, the lowest value, an interval of values, a missing value, and a system-missing value, respectively.

Example

```
COUNT MISSINGS = MARITALSTAT MOVEOUT (MISSING) WORKHOURS (999).
```

This creates a new variable called MISSINGS that contains the number of invalid or missing scores (MISSING and SYSMIS) on the indicated variables (see Section 3.7 on p. 28 for an explanation of the difference between MISSING and SYSMIS). The value 999 is counted as an invalid score for the variable WORKHOURS. Please note that the value 999 is not defined as a missing value and therefore is not recognized as such by SPSS. If you want to calculate the correct sample mean of the variable WORKHOURS, you will first have to turn the score 999 missing (invalid score); see p. 28–29 for an example (Table 3.7).

Results

```
FREQUENCIES
 /VARIABLES MISSINGS.
```

Table 3.7 Number of Respondents With 0 (1786), 1 (159), 2 (27), or 3 (2) "missings" on MARITALSTAT, MOVEOUT, and/or WORKHOURS

MISSINGS		Frequency	Percent	Valid Percent	Cumulative Percent
Valid	.00	1786	90.5	90.5	90.5
	1.00	159	8.1	8.1	98.5
	2.00	27	1.4	1.4	99.9
	3.00	2	.1	.1	100.0
	Total	1974	100.0	100.0	

3.12 IF △

Function

The IF command is used to assign values to a (new) variable when certain conditions are met. Suppose you want to construct a nominal variable "family composition" including the following categories: "unmarried without children," "married without children," "unmarried with children," and "married with children." You can achieve this with two variables: (1) being married (yes/no) and (2) having children (yes/no). From the combinations no-no, yes-no, no-yes, and yes-yes, the four categories of the new variable "family composition" can be constructed using the IF command (also see http://www.ru.nl/mt/syntax/home under "IF command").

Structure

A condition in parentheses follows the IF command. A brief explanation of these conditions can be found in the section on logical expressions (p. 13) and for a more extensive explanation, we refer you to the appendix (p. 121). The condition is followed by the variable name, a value, and an equal sign (=), and finally, the new value. The variable is constructed if it does not already exist, while all units of analysis (i.e., respondents) for which this condition does not apply will be assigned a "system missing" for this variable (see p. 28 for an explanation for "missing"). All other units will, of course, get the value that was indicated in the IF command.

Example

```
COMPUTE DECREASE = 0.
IF (CHURCHNOW < CHURCH15) DECREASE = 1.
```

In this example, a variable is constructed that indicates a decrease in church attendance during one's life. First, the variable is set to 0 for all respondents, which, in this case, refers to respondents who do not attend church less nowadays than they did at 15 years of age. The IF command will assign the value 1 to all respondents who at the time of the interview attended church less than when they were 15 years old (Table 3.8).

Results

```
FREQUENCIES
  /VARIABLES DECREASE.
```

Table 3.8 Frequency Distribution of the Variable DECREASE

DECREASE				
		Frequency	Percent	Valid Percent	Cumulative Percent
Valid	.00	1183	59.9	59.9	59.9
	1.00	791	40.1	40.1	100.0
	Total	1974	100.0	100.0	

△ 3.13 WRITE

Function

The WRITE command is used to store data (as in Section 3.3; see p. 23). The difference, however, is that the SAVE command saves data in the SPSS format (.sav), which most programs cannot open. WRITE will save data as a universal readable text file. This file contains one or more lines for each respondent on which the values of the variables are lined up in a row. The command is mostly used to save data files to programs that can read these text (ASCII) files.

Structure

The OUTFILE subcommand follows the WRITE command with the name of the file that is to be saved, a slash, the variables, and the format in which the file needs to be saved. Specifying the format is necessary because the values should now appear separated from each other by a (column) space or spaces. If left out, SPSS will produce a file wherein all the values of the variables are presented in a row without spaces, which is practically of no use. The variable format is indicated in parentheses prior to the variable name. This "description" starts with a letter indicating the type of variable. An "f" indicates a numerical variable, and an "a" indicates a string variable (e.g., the name of the place of residence). This is followed by a value that indicates the number of characters used by the variable. Always add one extra to the number of characters the variable needs, so that the variables are separated by a space. For a variable value with decimals, a period is placed after the figure indicating the number of characters, followed by the number of digits after the dot. The number −16.589, for example, is written as f8.3. There are eight positions necessary for this number: one space (to separate it from the former variable), the minus sign, two digits, a dot (separation sign for the decimals), and three decimals. The space can also be indicated by adding "1x" (see example). The file that is created with the WRITE command is only saved after the EXECUTE command or when a statistical procedure is executed (see p. 26).

Example

```
WRITE OUTFILE "c:/data/example.txt"
/IDNO (f4) SEX (f2) RELIGION (f5.2, 1x) SURVEY (a6).
EXECUTE.
```

In this example, the file "example.txt" is saved containing the variables in the command separated by spaces. The "(f4)" of IDNO indicates that four columns are used by this variable. The variable IDNO from the file "chapter3.sav" indeed covers up to four digits, and there is no need for a space to separate, because it is the first variable in the file. The variable SEX is separated from IDNO by a space, hence "f2" (1 space and 1 digit: 0 or 1 in this case). The variable RELIGION (a Likert scale) consists of four digits, two behind the dot, and needs an extra space to be separated from the variable SEX; therefore it is written as "f5.2." "1x" is added to ensure the space between RELIGION and SURVEY. The variable SURVEY indicates the specific version of the survey and consists of a string with a code (there were two versions of the survey, denoted as 1995A and 1995B). Because this variable uses six positions, it has to be written as "a6." It is not possible to write "a7" to create a space between RELIGION and SURVEY. You can open the file "example.txt" with a word processing program, like WordPad, Notepad, or Word. This command will create a file containing a table with four variables per respondent (see Table 3.9). Use the DATA LIST command to open the file in SPSS and check whether the command was properly executed (see Section 3.14).

Table 3.9 "example.txt" Opened in Word

```
 1  1  1.20  1995BP

 2  2   .00  1995AP

 3  2  1.00  1995BP

 7  2   .80  1995B

10  2  1.25  1995AP

11  1   .00  1995BP

13  1  1.20  1995BP

15  2   .80  1995BP
```

Note: The first eight rows are shown.

△ 3.14 DATA LIST

Function

The GET command (see p. 21) cannot open a text file with respondent information listed without formatting codes (e.g., when the file is made with WRITE; see p. 38). This command will only open .sav files. The DATA LIST command, however, can open such text files, but it has to be clearly specified how the file is to be opened, as it only contains numbers, without any information regarding what the number means.

Structure

The DATA LIST command is followed by the FILE subcommand, with the name of the file that is to be opened specified as a string. The file name is followed by a slash, and the variable names that are to be read from the file, as well as the format in which they are stored in the file. (See Section 3.13 (p. 38) for more information on the variable formats.) The syntax used for writing the data (see the WRITE command) can also be used to open the file. You only have to replace WRITE with DATA LIST (see the example below). The data will be displayed following the EXECUTE command or the execution of a statistical procedure (see p. 26) (Figure 3.5).

Example

```
DATA LIST FILE "c:/data/example.txt"
 /IDNO (f4) SEX (f2) RELIGION (f5.2, 1x) SURVEY (a6).
EXECUTE.
```

Note: This example requires the use of the file saved using the WRITE command (see Section 3.13).

Results

Figure 3.5 The File "example.txt" Opened With DATA LIST (First Eight Rows)

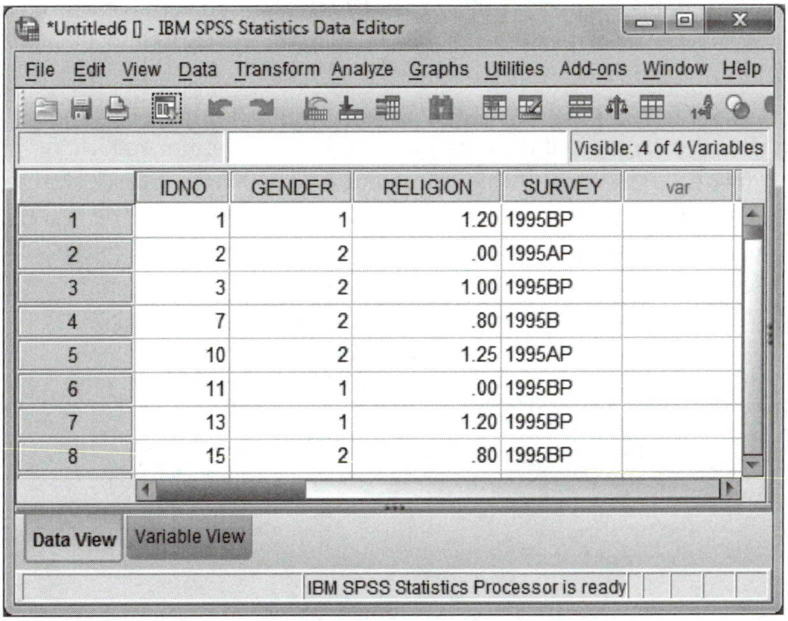

	IDNO	GENDER	RELIGION	SURVEY	var
1	1	1	1.20	1995BP	
2	2	2	.00	1995AP	
3	3	2	1.00	1995BP	
4	7	2	.80	1995B	
5	10	2	1.25	1995AP	
6	11	1	.00	1995BP	
7	13	1	1.20	1995BP	
8	15	2	.80	1995BP	

Note: The next section requires the use of the file "chapter3.sav"; please execute the GET command from Section 3.2 again.

△ 3.15 DO IF/ELSE IF/ELSE/END IF

Function

The DO IF command marks the beginning of a set of commands that are only executed if the condition behind the DO IF command is true. END IF marks the end of the set. The command resembles the IF command (p. 37), but instead of only assigning a value to a variable, a variety of data transformations can be executed here. This command is not meant to select respondents for analysis. (For more details, see sections 3.16, p. 44), and 3.17, p. 45.) The accompanying ELSE IF and ELSE commands specify transformations that will be executed when the condition behind DO IF is not true.

Structure

The command *always* starts with DO IF, followed by a logical expression in parentheses (for an explanation on logical expressions see p. 13 and the appendix on p. 121). The DO IF command ends with a period. This is followed by the transformations to be executed for respondents who meet the condition in the logical expression. Last, DO IF is closed with END IF. It is also possible, however, to add more transformations by including ELSE IF followed by the expression in parentheses, before you use the END IF command. You can even use more than one ELSE IF command. The commands in ELSE IF are executed if the conditions before this command have not been true while the condition of this command is true. Finally, before closing the END IF command, you can add ELSE (without a condition). The commands in ELSE will be executed for all respondents with yet unmet conditions. You can use this construction for recoding or saving the data of separate groups with WRITE (p. 38)—for example, multisampling analysis in LISREL.

Note: The whole structure between DO IF and END IF has to be executed at once. If only partly executed, later commands may become part of the DO IF command. We recommend finishing the whole DO IF/END IF command with EXECUTE, so that you can be sure the data transformations are actually executed.

Example

```
DO IF (EDUC < 3).
 WRITE OUTFILE "c:/data/low.txt"
```

```
/VOTES (f3) SEX(f2).
ELSE IF (EDUC < 5).
 WRITE OUTFILE "c:/data/middle.txt"
 / VOTES (f3) SEX (f2).
ELSE.
 WRITE OUTFILE "c:/data/high.txt"
 / VOTES (f3) SEX (f2).
END IF.
EXECUTE.
```

The commands write the variables VOTES and SEX to three separate files depending on the respondent's educational level. The command DO IF ensures that only respondents with a score lower than 3 on EDUC will be placed in the "low.txt" file. The ELSE IF command selects respondents with a score lower than 5 on EDUC. Because the respondents with a score lower than 3 are already placed in the "low.txt" file, only respondents with scores 3 and 4 will be placed in "middle.txt." Respondents with a score of 5 and higher are the only ones left, and consequently are placed in the "high.txt" file, with the ELSE command. The block ends with END IF, and EXECUTE ensures that the transformations are actually made. Please note that the WRITE command is indented with two spaces. The advantage of this is that it is immediately clear what transformations are associated with each condition.

Results

The three files can be opened again using DATA LIST (Section 3.14). The male/female distribution of the opened "middle.txt" file is displayed below (Table 3.10).

```
DATA LIST FILE "c:/Data/middle.txt"
 /VOTES (f3) SEX (f2).
FREQUENCIES SEX.
```

Table 3.10   Male/Female Distribution in the File "middle.txt"

SEX				
	Frequency	**Percent**	**Valid Percent**	**Cumulative Percent**
Valid 1	287	46.9	46.9	46.9
2	325	53.1	53.1	100.0
Total	612	100.0	100.0	

Note: The file "chapter3.sav" will be used in the next section; please execute the GET command from Section 3.2 again.

△ 3.16 SELECT IF

Function

SELECT IF is used to delete respondents *permanently* from the data file. All respondents (cases) who do not meet a certain condition are removed from the file. This could be useful to limit the data to a subset of respondents or to remove respondents with extreme scores (so-called outliers). However, the disadvantage of using this command is that if you save the new data file, the data of the excluded are deleted for good. For that reason, the TEMPORARY (Section 3.20, p. 49) and FILTER (Section 3.17, p. 45) commands can be used to temporarily exclude respondents instead.

Structure

A logical expression (see p. 13 and p. 121) in parentheses follows SELECT IF. All respondents who do not meet that condition are excluded (you can make this visible in the data window after running an EXECUTE command!).

Example

```
SELECT IF (SEX = 1).
EXECUTE.
```

The above command restricts future data operations and statistical analyses to all males only in the data file (Table 3.11).

Results

FREQUENCIES
/VARIABLES EDUC.

Table 3.11 Frequency Distribution of EDUC After Selecting Men Only

educ highest completed education				
	Frequency	**Percent**	**Valid Percent**	**Cumulative Percent**
1 Elementary school	72	7.6	7.6	7.6
2 Middle school	170	18.0	18.0	25.6
3 Junior high school	83	8.8	8.8	34.4
4 Senior high school	204	21.6	21.6	56.0
5 Vocational school	50	5.3	5.3	61.3
6 College	79	8.4	8.4	69.6
7 Bachelor degrees	191	20.2	20.2	89.8
8 Master degrees	96	10.2	10.2	100.0
Total	945	100.0	100.0	

Note: The file "chapter3.sav" will be used for the next section; execute the GET command from Section 3.2 again.

3.17 FILTER △

Function

The FILTER command is used to select respondents temporarily. They are not excluded permanently from the data file, as they are with SELECT IF (p. 44). The respondents remain inactive but can be reactivated in future analyses. As this command is executed immediately, there is no need for the EXECUTE command.

Structure

The BY operator follows the FILTER command to select a certain group and is then followed by the name of a variable. All respondents who score a 0, a missing, or an invalid (missing) value on this variable become inactive and are therefore excluded from further analyses. If the filter variable does not exist at this point, it must be created with COMPUTE (p. 34). All respondents are reactivated with the command FILTER OFF. If this command is omitted, all further analyses and transformations performed will be done with the selected respondents only!

Example

```
* calculate MALE with value 0 for women and 1 for men.
COMPUTE MALE = (SEX = 1).
FILTER BY MALE.
FREQUENCIES
 /VARIABLES EDUC.
FILTER OFF.
```

The COMPUTE statement has created the variable MALE, with a value of 1 indicating men and a value of 0 indicating women (see the appendix on logical expressions on p. 121 for an explanation of these types of constructions). The data file has then been filtered on this variable, activating only the male respondents. The following command is only executed for men— the frequency distribution for educational level in this case. Finally, the filter is turned off again with FILTER OFF. The results of the example are equal to the results of the previous section (see Table 3.11).

△ 3.18 SORT CASES

Function

The SORT CASES command sorts respondents on one or more variables. This is especially useful because some commands (i.e., see sections 3.19 on p. 48, and 3.21 on p. 51) and certain programs (e.g., MLwiN) require the data to be sorted. Sometimes, it is also useful to have the respondents in a particular order to inspect the data yourself. As this command is executed immediately, there is no need for the EXECUTE command.

Structure

SORT CASES is followed by the BY operator and then by one or more variable names. If only one variable is specified, the data are simply sorted on that variable. If multiple variables are specified, respondents who score the same value on the first variable will be sorted on the second variable, respondents who score the same value on the second variable will be sorted on the third variable, and so on. The respondents are sorted in ascending order by default: lowest scores appear first, while higher scores appear last. Respondents can be sorted in descending order by adding "(D)" after the name of the variable.

Example

SORT CASES BY REGION (D) PROVINCE.

The command has sorted respondents by regions and provinces. The region codes are sorted in descending order and the province codes in ascending order (see Figure 3.6).

Results

Figure 3.6 File Sorted for REGION (D) and PROVINCE (Rows 236 to 243 Are Shown)

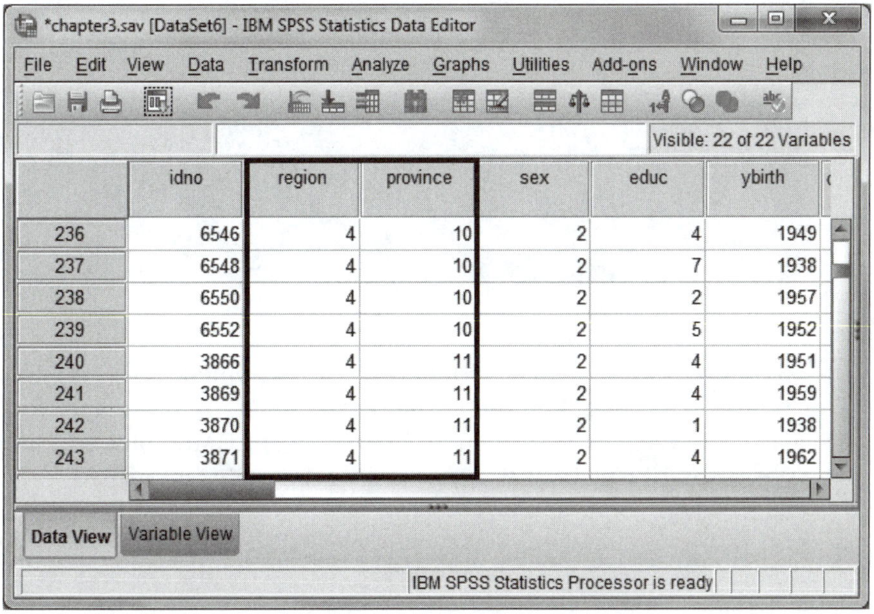

	idno	region	province	sex	educ	ybirth
236	6546	4	10	2	4	1949
237	6548	4	10	2	7	1938
238	6550	4	10	2	2	1957
239	6552	4	10	2	5	1952
240	3866	4	11	2	4	1951
241	3869	4	11	2	4	1959
242	3870	4	11	2	1	1938
243	3871	4	11	2	4	1962

△ 3.19 SPLIT FILE

Function

SPLIT FILE splits the respondents into groups and separately analyses them. When, for example, the samples of men and women are split, statistical analyses for men and women are done separately. Splitting a file is therefore mainly used when comparing groups, for example, with histograms or frequency distributions.

Structure

First, the data have to be sorted on the variables that are used to split the file. You can use the SORT CASES command for this (see p. 46). After that the SPLIT FILE is followed by the operator BY and the name of the variable that is going to be split. It is also possible to split the file by multiple variables—the file must be sorted on all variables for this! The outcome of a split command is that statistical information for *every combination* of categories of those variables is displayed. If the variables have many categories (e.g., age), then this can lead to cluttered results. The split is turned off by the SPLIT FILE OFF command.

Example

```
SORT CASES BY SEX.
SPLIT FILE BY SEX.
FREQUENCIES CHURCHMEMBER.
SPLIT FILE OFF.
```

The example is first sorted by SEX: first men (Value 1) followed by women (Value 2). Then, the file is split by SEX, and for both males and females, the frequencies for CHURCHMEMBER are displayed (see FREQUENCIES, p. 75). Finally, the split is turned off again (Table 3.12).

Results

Table 3.12 Separate Frequency Distributions of Church Membership for Men and Women

Church membership				
Sex		Frequency	Percent	Valid Percent	Cumulative Percent
1 Male	1 Yes	364	38.5	38.5	38.5
	2 No	558	59.0	59.0	97.6
	3 Don't know/ unsure	20	2.1	2.1	99.7
	99 Not applicable	3	.3	.3	100.0
	Total	945	100.0	100.0	
2 Female	1 Yes	454	44.1	44.1	44.1
	2 No	550	53.4	53.4	97.6
	3 Don't know/ unsure	20	1.9	1.9	99.5
	99 Not applicable	5	.5	.5	100.0
	Total	1029	100.0	100.0	

3.20 TEMPORARY △

Function

The TEMPORARY command is used to execute the subsequent command temporarily. This transformation is undone *after* a second command is executed. TEMPORARY can be used in combination with MISSING VALUES (p. 28), RECODE (p. 32), COMPUTE (p. 34), COUNT (p. 35), IF (p. 37), SELECT IF (p. 44), FILTER (p. 45), and SPLIT FILE (p. 48). This means that the changes these commands make in the file only apply to the following command. TEMPORARY is typically combined with SELECT IF to ensure that the selection is not permanent. TEMPORARY does not have subcommands.

Example

```
TEMPORARY.
SELECT IF (REGION = 2).
FREQUENCIES SEX.
FREQUENCIES SEX.
```

Normally, the SELECT IF command deletes every respondent who does not meet the condition in the file. However, when it is combined with TEMPORARY, the selection is only applied to the subsequent command. The first FREQUENCIES command (see p. 75) is only executed for respondents living in Region 2 (the east). The second FREQUENCIES command, however, applies to all respondents. Thus, the results display a frequency distribution by SEX for respondents living in Region 2 (east) and a frequency distribution by SEX for all respondents (all regions) (Tables 3.13 and 3.14).

Results

Table 3.13 Frequency Distribution of Sex for Region 2

		Frequency	Percent	Valid Percent	Cumulative Percent
Valid	1 Male	213	48.3	48.3	48.3
	2 Female	228	51.7	51.7	100.0
	Total	441	100.0	100.0	

Table 3.14 Frequency Distribution of Sex for All Regions

		Frequency	Percent	Valid Percent	Cumulative Percent
Valid	1 Male	945	47.9	47.9	47.9
	2 Female	1029	52.1	52.1	100.0
	Total	1974	100.0	100.0	

3.21 MATCH FILES △

Function

MATCH FILES is typically used to connect variables and/or units from different data sets. There are two ways to do this. First, files can contain (a lot of) the same units of analysis (often respondents), but with different sets of variables. If this is the case, the files are set up side by side. The units of analysis are recognized by their identification numbers, and the variables from all data sets will be assigned to each unit (respondent). Second, it is possible that one or more of the data sets you want to match contain different units of analysis, that is, countries or regions. When, for instance, you want to match a file where respondents are the units of analysis with a file where regions are the units of analysis, the respondents need to have a region code. The files can then be matched on these region codes, so that the characteristics of the regions—such as unemployment rates or population statistics—can be linked to the respondents from that region.

Structure

To successfully match the files, they have to be sorted (in ascending order; see Section 3.18, p. 46) by the variable(s) that identify the units of analysis. This variable (called the *key variable*) should be present in all files to be matched. When using data where respondents are the units of analysis, the key variable is usually the respondent identifier, which is a unique code. When a file contains information on regions, the region code is the key variable. After sorting the files, the MATCH FILES command can be used, followed by the FILE subcommand with the name of the first file (the file where the respondents are the units). If the file has not been opened yet, it can be indicated by a string value with the file name or just with an asterisk (*) if the current (active) file has to be used. Next, the second file has to be indicated. When both files contain the same units of analysis (e.g., respondents), the FILE subcommand can be used again, this time with the file name of the second file. However, the second file can also contain information on "higher" units of analysis. For instance, the units of the first file (respondents) can be clustered in units of the second file, such as regions or countries. If that is the case, the TABLE subcommand has to be used instead of FILE. The subcommands FILE and TABLE can be repeated, should you need to match more files. After specifying all the files, the BY subcommand is used, followed by the key variable. There could be more than one key variable: for instance, the variables "region" and "time," if you have information for all regions on unemployment rates for every year in the 1980–2006 period. When more than one key variable is used, the files have to be sorted in ascending order by all these variables. Please note that the order in which the key variables are sorted and the order of the variables in the BY subcommand have to be the same!

Example

```
SORT CASES BY PROVINCE.
MATCH FILES FILE *
/TABLE "c:/data/provinces.sav"
/BY PROVINCE.
EXECUTE.
```

In this example, the variable NOCHURCH (the percentage of non–church members in a province) is added from the file "provinces.sav" to the individual data from the opened file "chapter3.sav." The location of the file "provinces.sav" is specified after the TABLE command. This file was already sorted by the variable PROVINCE. The active file is sorted by the SORT CASES command. The new, matched data are only visible after using the EXECUTE command (p. 26).

Result

```
SPLIT FILE BY PROVINCE.
FREQUENCIES NOCHURCH.
SPLIT FILE OFF.
```

To check whether the match was successful, the percentage of non–church members per province in the Netherlands is required (Table 3.15a).

Table 3.15a Percentage of Non–Church Members per Province

Province Where the Respondents Were Interviewed	Frequency	Percent	Valid Percent	Cumulative Percent
1 Groningen	76.90	64	100.0	100.0
2 Friesland	63.70	105	100.0	100.0
3 Drenthe	62.10	48	100.0	100.0
4 Overijssel	53.90	107	100.0	100.0
5 Gelderland	59.20	295	100.0	100.0
6 Utrecht	61.20	56	100.0	100.0
7 Noord-Holland	77.60	283	100.0	100.0
8 Zuid-Holland	63.60	464	100.0	100.0
9 Zeeland	53.00	91	100.0	100.0
10 Noord-Brabant	56.50	239	100.0	100.0
11 Limburg	43.10	186	100.0	100.0
12 Flevoland	45.20	36	100.0	100.0

Optional Subcommands

The RENAME subcommand can be used in the command as well. This is especially useful when the key variable does not have the same name in all files. RENAME is used after the FILE or TABLE subcommand with the variable that needs to be renamed. One or more name changes follow the RENAME command. This includes the old variable name, an equal sign (=), and the new variable name, all within parentheses ().

As with the GET command (p. 21), variables can be excluded by the subcommands KEEP or DROP. These follow the BY subcommand. KEEP is followed by a list of variables that you want to include in the final file. The variables that follow the DROP command are those that you want to exclude from the final file.

Extensive Example

```
MATCH FILES FILE="c:\data\chapter3.sav"
/FILE "c:/data/chapter3match.sav"
/RENAME (v0038= child)
/FILE "c:/Data/chapter3match2.sav"
/BY IDNO
/DROP REGION PROVINCE.
```

In this example, three files are matched, each containing information on respondents. Two extra operations (RENAME and DROP) have been included here. First, the "chapter3.sav" file is opened, and second the "chapter3match.sav" file with the same respondents is opened. The latter file contains a variable V0038, which is renamed as CHILD. Please note that RENAME follows the command that opens the "chapter3match.sav" file, because this is what the RENAME command refers to. Next, the "chapter3match2.sav" file is opened, which contains information on the respondent's partner. The three files are matched, excluding two variables REGION and PROVINCE.

Result

```
FREQUENCIES CHILD PARTNER.
FREQUENCIES CHILD REGION PROVINCE.
```

The above command displays the frequency distribution of the number of children (CHILD) and whether the respondent has a partner. The last line in the command box requests the frequency distribution of CHILD, REGION, and PROVINCE. A warning will follow in the output because the latter two variables no longer exist, indicating that the DROP operation was effective (Tables 3.15b and c).

Table 3.15b Frequency Distribution of CHILD

child: number of children				
		Frequency	**Percent**	**Valid Percent**	**Cumulative Percent**
Valid	0	675	34.2	34.2	34.2
	1	232	11.8	11.8	45.9
	2	614	31.1	31.1	77.1
	3	303	15.3	15.3	92.4
	4	87	4.4	4.4	96.8
	5	33	1.7	1.7	98.5
	6	17	.9	.9	99.3
	7	4	.2	.2	99.5
	8	4	.2	.2	99.7
	9	5	.3	.3	100.0
	Total	1974	100.0	100.0	

Table 3.15c Frequency Distribution of PARTNER and a Warning for REGION and PROVINCE

partner has got a partner				
		Frequency	**Percent**	**Valid Percent**	**Cumulative Percent**
Valid	1 Yes	1449	73.4	73.4	73.4
	2 No	525	26.6	26.6	100.0
	Total	1974	100.0	100.0	

Warnings
Text: REGION Command: FREQUENCIES
An undefined variable name, or a scratch or system variable was specified in a variable list that accepts only standard variables. Check spelling and verify the existence of this variable.
Execution of this command stops.
Text: PROVINCE Command: FREQUENCIES
An undefined variable name, or a scratch or system variable was specified in a variable list that accepts only standard variables. Check spelling and verify the existence of this variable.

△ 3.22 ADD FILES

Function

The ADD FILES command is used to group together unique respondents (cases) from different data files. The result is a new data file in which the original files are placed one after the other. As a consequence, the total number of cases in the new file equals the sum of the cases in all added files. The values from variables with the same name are placed under each other while the labels and definitions for the missing values are retrieved from the first file. Before files are merged this way, you have to make sure that a variable has exactly the same name in all data sets, as well as the same missing values and coding of categories, all of which may differ across the data sets, of course.

Structure

ADD FILES is followed by the subcommand FILE, and the directory and name of the first file. You can specify the file name as a string or use an asterisk (*) to specify that the active file is to be used. After that you can add the additional FILE commands specifying the files that need to be added to the first file. The file names are specified as a string in this case as well.

Example

```
ADD FILES FILE "c:\data\chapter3.sav"
/FILE "c:/data/chapter3add.sav"
/FILE "c:/data/chapter3add2.sav".
EXECUTE.
```

In this example, a total of 20 respondents from the files "chapter3add.sav" and "chapter3add2.sav" are added to the file "chapter3.sav," increasing the total number of respondents to 1994. The added files contain the same variables as in the original file, so there are no additional missing values. The EXECUTE command is necessary to visualize the new data in the data window (Table 3.16).

Results

FREQUENCIES SEX.

Table 3.16 Frequency Distribution of Sex After Adding 20 Respondents

		Frequency	Percent	Valid Percent	Cumulative Percent
Sex					
Valid	1 Male	955	47.9	47.9	47.9
	2 Female	1039	52.1	52.1	100.0
	Total	1994	100.0	100.0	

Optional Subcommands

With RENAME positioned after the FILE subcommand, you can specify that some variables need to be renamed first. For each variable, specify the variable name in parentheses, followed by an equal sign (=), and finally the new name. With KEEP and DROP, you can specify which variables are kept or dropped, respectively, in the new data file.

Note: The next section requires the "chapter3.sav" file again (so execute the GET command from Section 3.2 again).

3.23 DO REPEAT/END REPEAT △

Function

The DO REPEAT command is generally used for reducing the number of commands, for instance, when you have to compute a lot of new variables. It can also be applied to the recoding of many variables at the same time. It saves time and reduces possible errors when only using this command instead of all the repetitions. To illustrate, we will create dummy variables that are coded 0 and 1, and are often used in linear regression analysis.

Structure

Following DO REPEAT, the name of the so-called stand-in variable must be specified. This particular variable only exists within the DO REPEAT command and represents all variables or numbers that follow this variable. After the stand-in variable, just type the equal sign (=) and then the list with variables (existing or nonexisting) or numbers. The names you use, of course, must follow the syntax rules (see Section 2.2).

Existing variables that stand next to each other in the data matrix can be listed using TO. For instance, V1 TO V15 will include all 15 existing variables (provided no other variables lie in between). Similarly, we can generate a whole list of nonexisting variables. The command V1NEW TO V15NEW creates 15 new variables. The syntax operator TO can also be used to generate a series of numbers, such as "1 TO 20." With a forward slash (/), we can generate a second series of variables or numbers. Note that the series must be of equal length, so the first series "V1 TO V15" must be followed by "1 TO 15." Within the DO REPEAT structure, almost all commands to modify data can be used, but no commands that run statistical analyses. The structure is closed by the END REPEAT subcommand to signify that all enclosed commands end here. The results are visible in the data window following EXECUTE or a command that implies EXECUTE such as FREQUENCIES.

Example

```
DO REPEAT DUMMY = ELEMENT MIDDLE JUNIOR SENIOR
VOCATIONAL COLLEGE BACHELOR MASTER
/NUMBER = 1 TO 8.
   IF (EDUC = NUMBER) DUMMY=1.
   IF (EDUC <> NUMBER) DUMMY=0.
END REPEAT.
```

In this example, eight dummy variables are created for all eight educational levels in the variable EDUC (this variable measures the highest attained educational level). For each level, a unique variable is created that has the value 1 for all respondents who attained that particular level and a value of 0 for all respondents who attained another level. We use two series in the DO REPEAT structure. The first is a series of eight new variables that are labeled (1) ELEMENT, (2) MIDDLE, (3) JUNIOR, (4) SENIOR, (5) VOCATIONAL, (6) COLLEGE, (7) BACHELOR, and (8) MASTER. Please note that we hold on to the rules for naming variables in SPSS (see Section 2.2). The second series also has eight elements, but this time it contains the numbers 1 to 8.

Within the DO REPEAT/END REPEAT structure, the two IF commands (see p. 37) are repeated (or "run") 8 times. In the first run, the variable "ELEMENT" is created together with "Number," which is set to 1. So the first IF command reads as follows: If (EDUC = 1) ELEMENT = 1. This means that all respondents with elementary school (coded 1 in EDUC) get the value 1 in the variable ELEMENT. The second IF command reads as follows: IF (EDUC <> 1) ELEMENT=0. So all respondents with scores other than 1 in EDUC score a 0 on ELEMENT. In the data set, we have four respondents with no valid score (so-called missings)—they will automatically receive a missing value as well in this structure. This makes sense because we do not know their highest attained educational level, and so none of the dummy variables apply here.

In a second run, the dummy variable changes to MIDDLE while the NUMBER variable now equals 2. So the IF commands are as follows: IF (EDUC=2) MIDDLE=1 and IF (EDUC <> 2) MIDDLE=0. So all respondents with middle school (code 2 in EDUC) receive a value of 1 in the variable MIDDLE, while all other respondents (save the four with a missing value) receive a 0 for this dummy variable. In the next six runs, the six remaining levels are treated likewise. When you have many variables that need recoding, this structure is most useful. Furthermore, it reduces the risk of making errors. However, as always, do not forget to run all necessary checks (for results, see Table 3.17).

Results

Note: Only tables for EDUC and ELEMENT are shown.

```
FREQUENCIES
 /VARIABLES EDUC ELEMENT MIDDLE JUNIOR SENIOR
VOCATIONAL COLLEGE BACHELOR MASTER.
```

Table 3.17   Frequency Distribution for Education and "ELEMENT"

educ highest completed education				
	Frequency	**Percent**	**Valid Percent**	**Cumulative Percent**
1 Elementary school	215	10.9	10.9	10.9
2 Middle school	338	17.1	17.2	28.1
3 Junior high school	220	11.1	11.2	39.2
4 Senior high school	392	19.9	19.9	59.1
5 Vocational school	133	6.7	6.8	65.9
6 College	140	7.1	7.1	73.0
7 Bachelor degrees	388	19.7	19.7	92.7
8 Master degrees	144	7.3	7.3	100.0
Total	1970	99.8	100.0	
Missing system	4	.2		
Total	1974	100.0		

Check: The number of cases coded 1 in ELEMENT must be equal to 215, while the number of cases coded 0 in ELEMENT must equal 1,755 (1974 – 215 – 4).

ELEMENT					
		Frequency	**Percent**	**Valid Percent**	**Cumulative Percent**
Valid	.00	1755	88.9	89.1	89.1
	1.00	215	10.9	10.9	100.0
	Total	1970	99.8	100.0	
Missing system		4	.2		
Total		1974	100.0		

△ 3.24 LOOP

Function

The LOOP command resembles the DO REPEAT command (p. 57) with respect to the repetition of a number of commands that are executed for each line (each respondent) in a single run. The LOOP command is more flexible, however, which makes it possible to construct more complex data structures such as an "event history" file in which you can follow the life course of respondents.

Structure

When a procedure needs to be executed a number of times, the LOOP command is followed by the name of the variable called the *index*. If the name of the index variable is preceded by a "#," the index variable is a temporary variable. The equal sign (=) follows the name, then the starting value, the word TO, and the end value. "LOOP #NUMBER = 1 TO 10" means that SPSS will run the LOOP 10 times for each respondent. During the run, the value of the variable #NUMBER increases by 1 for every run. If the variable has to increase by a value other than 1, for instance, 2 or even −1 (counting backward), the BY operator can be added + a number that indicates the value that the index variable has to increase (positive number) or decrease (negative number). The END LOOP command is placed at the end of the block to indicate the end of the loop. The EXECUTE command must be used to execute the LOOP.

Example

In the example below, a loop is run 100 times, and for each time, the age (starting with age = 1) and the identification number (IDNO) is written in the outfile with XSAVE.[2] To check whether the file is correct, we use the GET FILE command (p. 21). In the example below, a life-course file is constructed in which each respondent gets a data line for each year of his or her life between 1 year and 100 years (Figure 3.7a).

```
LOOP #NUMBER = 1 TO 100.
 COMPUTE AGE2 = #number.
 XSAVE OUTFILE = "c:/data/age.sav"
 /keep=IDNO AGE2.
END LOOP.
EXECUTE.
```

---

[2]XSAVE is similar to SAVE (see p. 23); however, with XSAVE data can be saved during an operation (such as LOOP). This is not possible with SAVE.

Results

```
GET FILE = "c:/data/age.sav".
EXECUTE.
```

Figure 3.7a   The Last 7 Years of Respondent 1 and the First 7 Years of Respondent 2 From "age.sav"

Extensive Example

With respect to the life-course file, we generally follow all respondents from a certain age until the age at the time of the interview. To this end, a DO IF/ END IF command (p. 42) is placed in the LOOP command. It is also possible to include variables that contain information about respondents at a certain age with the IF command (p. 37).

Note: First open the "chapter3.sav" file before running the syntax below!

```
LOOP #NUMBER = 1 TO 100.
COMPUTE AGE2 = #NUMBER.
DO IF (AGE2 > 11) and (AGE2<= (1995 − YBIRTH)).
COMPUTE SELF = 0.
```

```
  IF (MOVEOUT <= AGE2) SELF=1.
  XSAVE OUTFILE = "c:/data/age2.sav"
   /keep=IDNO SEX AGE2 SELF.
  END IF.
END LOOP.
EXECUTE.
```

A record is written for every year of a respondent's life into "age2.sav." In this file, age starts at 12 and ends with the respondent's age in 1995 (see the DO IF command and note the positioning of the END IF command!). Furthermore, the variable SELF is calculated to indicate whether the respondent was living at the parental home at a certain age (SELF=0) or left the parental home (SELF=1). This variable is written to the "age2.sav" file, together with the variables IDNO, SEX, and AGE (see Figure 3.7b).

Results

```
GET FILE = "c:/data/age2.sav".
EXECUTE.
```

Figure 3.7b Life Course of Respondent 1 Between the Age of 12 and 19 Years (Left Parental Home Since the Age of 18); Data From "age2.sav"

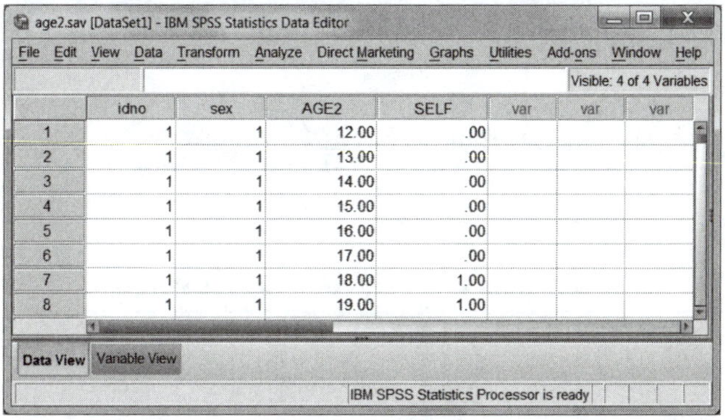

	idno	sex	AGE2	SELF	var	var	var
1	1	1	12.00	.00			
2	1	1	13.00	.00			
3	1	1	14.00	.00			
4	1	1	15.00	.00			
5	1	1	16.00	.00			
6	1	1	17.00	.00			
7	1	1	18.00	1.00			
8	1	1	19.00	1.00			

Note: The "chapter3.sav" file has to be opened for the next section (so execute the GET command from Section 3.2 again).

△ 3.25 WEIGHT

Function

The command WEIGHT can be used in two ways: (1) to eliminate under- or overrepresentation in a sample or (2) to analyze a data file where one data record refers to several respondents simultaneously. Such files can save a lot of time compared with putting all units in individual records (see the second example in "chapter3weight.sav").

Structure

WEIGHT is followed by the subcommand BY and the name of the weight variable (also called weight factor). End the syntax file with WEIGHT OFF to undo the weighting (Table 3.18).

Results

```
* First example: weighting to correct ratio.
* In the population the male-female ratio is 49.5/50.5.
* In chapter3.sav that ratio is 47.9 / 52.1.
IF SEX EQ 1 SEXRATIO=49.5/47.9.
IF SEX EQ 2 SEXRATIO=50.5/52.1.
WEIGHT BY SEXRATIO.
FREQUENCIES
 /VARIABLES SEX.
WEIGHT OFF.
```

Table 3.18 The Male-Female Ratio After Weighting

Sex		Frequency	Percent	Valid Percent	Cumulative Percent
Valid	1 Male	977	49.5	49.5	49.5
	2 Female	997	50.5	50.5	100.0
	Total	1974	100.0	100.0	

```
* Second example: analysis on a data file where a line represents more
than one respondent.
GET FILE "c:/Data/chapter3weight.sav".
WEIGHT BY NUMBER.
FREQUENCIES
 /VARIABLES SEX.
WEIGHT OFF.
```

Please take a look at the data structure of "chapter3weight.sav" and see Table 3.14 for checks on the results after weighting.

Note: The "chapter3.sav" file has to be opened for the next section (so execute the GET command from Section 3.2 again).

3.26 SAMPLE △

Function

SAMPLE is used to draw a random sample from a data file. This is useful when the data file is too large for analysis. This command is also used as a form of sensitivity analysis to check the stability of the results.

Structure

Following SAMPLE, a proportion is given (e.g., .25) or two numbers separated by FROM, where the first number specifies the exact number of cases required in the subsample, and the second number is normally equal to the sample size (e.g., 25 from 100) (Table 3.19).

Results of a 10% Sample

Note: Outcomes will differ for each draw.

```
SAMPLE .10.
FREQUENCIES
 /VARIABLES SEX.
```

Table 3.19 Random Sample of Approximately 10% From "chapter3.sav"

		Frequency	Percent	Valid Percent	Cumulative Percent
				Sex	
Valid	1 Male	87	44.8	44.8	44.8
	2 Female	107	55.2	55.2	100.0
	Total	194	100.0	100.0	

△ **3.27 SPSS Syntax: An Overview**

```
*** 3.2: opens the data file for third chapter.
GET FILE "c:/Data/chapter3.sav".
* Macintosh users: GET FILE "/data/chapter3.sav".

* opens the data file for third chapter, with DROP and RENAME.
GET FILE "c:/Data/chapter3.sav"
 /DROP LIST FUTURE
 /RENAME GOD2 = BELIEVE_NOW GOD1 = BELIEVE_15.
EXECUTE.

*** 3.3 saves the file.
SAVE OUTFILE "c:/Data/chapter3new.sav".
GET FILE "c:/Data/chapter3new.sav".

*** 3.3 saves file with KEEP and RENAME.
SAVE OUTFILE "c:/Data/chapter3short.sav"
 /KEEP SEX EDUC YBIRTH CHURCHMEMBER VOTES
 /RENAME VOTES = POLITICS.
GET FILE "c:/Data/chapter3short.sav".

* PLEASE NOTE: reopen data file for third chapter.
GET FILE "c:/Data/chapter3.sav".

*** 3.5 adds informative variable labels.
VARIABLE LABELS LEAVECHURCH "age at which the respondent left
church" YBIRTH "year of birth of the respondent".
FREQUENCIES
 VARIABLES=LEAVECHURCH YBIRTH.
```

```
*** 3.6 adds informative names for categories.
VALUE LABELS SEX 1 "Male" 2 "Female"
 /REGION 1 "North" 2 "East" 3 "West" 4 "South".
FREQUENCIES
 VARIABLES=SEX REGION.

*** 3.7 specifies missing values.
MISSING VALUES VOTES (14 15 16) CHURCHMEMBER
LEAVECHURCH (99).
*** undoes missing values.
MISSING VALUES HEAVEN ().
FREQUENCIES
 VARIABLES=LEAVECHURCH CHURCHMEMBER VOTES HEAVEN.

*** 3.8 displays variables.
DISPLAY DICTIONARY
 /VARIABLES SEX MARITALSTAT EDUC.

*** 3.9: recodes a variable.
RECODE VOTES (1 5 12 = 1) (2 4 9 10 = 2) (3 6 THRU 8 11 = 3)
 (ELSE = 999) INTO POLITICS.
FREQUENCIES
 VARIABLES=POLITICS.

*** 3.10: computes new variable.
COMPUTE OWNHOME = (1995 – YBIRTH) – MOVEOUT.
FREQUENCIES
 VARIABLES=OWNHOME
 /STATISTICS DEFAULT.

***3.11: counts scores.
COUNT MISSINGS = MARITALSTAT MOVEOUT (MISSING)
WORKHOURS (999).
FREQUENCIES
 VARIABLES=MISSINGS.

***3.12: constructs a new variable by a condition.
COMPUTE DECREASE = 0.
IF (CHURCHNOW < CHURCH15) DECREASE = 1.
FREQUENCIES VARIABLES=DECREASE.

***3.13: saves to a different type of data file.
WRITE OUTFILE "c:/Data/example.txt"
```

```
 /IDNO (f4) SEX (f2) RELIGION (f5.2, 1x) SURVEY (a6).
EXECUTE.

***3.14: reads txt type data file.
DATA LIST FILE "c:/Data/example.txt"
 /IDNO (f4) SEX (f2) RELIGION (f5.2, 1x) SURVEY (a6).
EXECUTE.

* PLEASE NOTE: open data file for third chapter again.
GET FILE "c:/Data/chapter3.sav".

***3.15: executes commands under condition.
DO IF (EDUC < 3).
 WRITE OUTFILE "c:/Data/low.txt"
 /VOTES (f3) SEX (f2).
ELSE IF (EDUC < 5).
 WRITE OUTFILE "c:/Data/middle.txt"
 /VOTES (f3) SEX (f2).
ELSE.
 WRITE OUTFILE "c:/Data/high.txt"
 /VOTES (f3) SEX (f2).
END IF.
EXECUTE.
DATA LIST FILE "c:/Data/middle.txt"
 /VOTES (f3) SEX (f2).
FREQUENCIES SEX.

*PLEASE NOTE: open data file for third chapter again.
GET FILE "c:/Data/chapter3.sav".

***3.16: (permanently) selecting cases.
SELECT IF (SEX = 1).
FREQUENCIES
 /VARIABLES EDUC.

*PLEASE NOTE: opening file for third chapter again.
GET FILE "c:/Data/chapter3.sav".

***3.17: (temporarily) selecting cases.
COMPUTE MALE = (SEX = 1).
FILTER BY MALE.
FREQUENCIES
 /VARIABLES EDUC.
FILTER OFF.
```

```
***3.18: sorts the data file.
SORT CASES BY REGION (D) PROVINCE.

***3.19: splits the data file.
SORT CASES BY SEX.
SPLIT FILE BY SEX.
FREQUENCIES CHURCHMEMBER.
SPLIT FILE OFF.

***3.20: temporarily executes selection and one analysis.
TEMPORARY.
SELECT IF (REGION = 2).
FREQUENCIES SEX.
FREQUENCIES SEX.

***3.21: matches files, example with file/table.
SORT CASES BY PROVINCE.
MATCH FILES FILE *
 /TABLE "c:/Data/provinces.sav"
 /BY PROVINCE.
EXECUTE.
SPLIT FILE BY PROVINCE.
FREQUENCIES NOCHURCH.
SPLIT FILE OFF.

* extensive example with file/file.
MATCH FILES FILE="c:\data\chapter3.sav"
 /FILE "c:/Data/chapter3match.sav"
 /RENAME (v0038= child)
 /FILE "c:/Data/chapter3match2.sav"
 /BY IDNO
 /DROP REGION PROVINCE.
EXECUTE.
FREQUENCIES CHILD PARTNER.
FREQUENCIES CHILD REGION PROVINCE.

*** 3.22: adding respondents.
ADD FILES FILE= "c:\data\chapter3.sav"
 /FILE "c:/Data/chapter3add.sav"
 /FILE "c:/Data/chapter3add2.sav".
EXECUTE.
FREQUENCIES SEX.
```

```
*PLEASE NOTE: open file for third chapter again.
GET FILE "c:/Data/chapter3.sav".

*** 3.23: makes dummy variables the easy way.
DO REPEAT DUMMY = ELEMENT MIDDLE JUNIOR SENIOR
                        VOCATIONAL COLLEGE BACHELOR MASTER
 /NUMBER = 1 TO 8.
IF (EDUC = NUMBER) DUMMY=1.
IF (EDUC <> NUMBER) DUMMY=0.
END REPEAT.
FREQUENCIES VARIABLES EDUC ELEMENT MIDDLE JUNIOR SENIOR
 VOCATIONAL COLLEGE BACHELOR MASTER.

***3.24: writes cases more than once.
LOOP #NUMBER = 1 TO 100.
 COMPUTE AGE2 = #NUMBER.
 XSAVE OUTFILE = "c:/data/age.sav" /keep=IDNO AGE2.
END LOOP.
EXECUTE.
GET FILE = "c:/data/age.sav".
EXECUTE.

*PLEASE NOTE: open data file for third chapter again.
GET FILE "c:/Data/chapter3.sav".

LOOP #NUMBER = 1 TO 100.
 COMPUTE AGE2 = #NUMBER.
 DO IF (AGE2 > 11) and (AGE2 <= (1995 − YBIRTH)).
 COMPUTE SELF = 0.
 IF (MOVEOUT <= AGE2) SELF=1.
 XSAVE OUTFILE = "c:/data/age2.sav"
 /keep=IDNO SEX AGE2 SELF.
 END IF.
END LOOP.
EXECUTE.
GET FILE = "c:/data/age2.sav".
EXECUTE.

*PLEASE NOTE: opening file for third chapter again.
GET FILE "c:/Data/chapter3.sav".
```

```
***3.25 weights to population.
* First example: weighting to correct proportions.
* The male/female ratio in the population is 49.5/50.5.
* In chapter3.sav this ratio is 47.9 / 52.1.
IF SEX EQ 1 SEXRATIO =49.5/47.9.
IF SEX EQ 2 SEXRATIO =50.5/52.1.
WEIGHT BY SEXRATIO.
FREQUENCIES
 /VARIABLES SEX.
WEIGHT OFF.

* Second example: analysis on data file in which a data row represents
more than one observation (respondent).
GET FILE "c:/Data/chapter3weight.sav".
WEIGHT BY NUMBER.
FREQUENCIES
 /VARIABLES SEX.
WEIGHT OFF.

*PLEASE NOTE: open file for third chapter again.
GET FILE "c:/Data/chapter3.sav".

*** 3.26 Random sampling.
SAMPLE .10.
FREQUENCIES /VARIABLES SEX.
```

Statistical Analyses

4.1 Introduction △

This chapter deals with the most common commands for statistical analyses. In the first sections, the emphasis is on simple descriptive analyses, while later sections discuss more advanced inferential analyses. Some theoretical statistical knowledge is essential before reading any sections that deal with unfamiliar statistical techniques. We recommend *Discovering Statistics Using SPSS* by Andy Field, a statistics textbook that requires little mathematical knowledge. Many of the subcommands discussed in this chapter are required only for specific situations. Thus, a need-based study of this chapter is recommended. Unlike in previous chapters, we sometimes discuss examples using the "paste" option from the menu when it is more efficient than typing in the syntax. Please first execute the "chapter4.sav" file for the data used in this chapter.

```
GET FILE "c:/data/chapter4.sav".
* Macintosh computers use: GET FILE "/data/chapter4.sav".
```

4.2 DESCRIPTIVES △

Function

DESCRIPTIVES calculates certain statistical characteristics of a variable, such as the mean, median, and standard deviation. This command is also used for standardizing variables through the z transformation, where the mean $= 0$ and the standard deviation $= 1$.

Structure

A variable, or a list of variables, follows the DESCRIPTIVES command. This displays the number of units of analysis with a valid score (N), minimum, maximum, mean, and standard deviation of the variable(s). The STATISTICS subcommand is used to specify other statistical measures. This subcommand is followed by the measures that you require. Common measures include the mean (MEAN), standard deviation (STDDEV), variance (VARIANCE), range (RANGE), minimum and maximum values (MINIMUM & MAXIMUM), and sum of all values (SUM). ALL retrieves all available measures (including standard error and skewness) (Table 4.1).

Example

```
DESCRIPTIVES YBIRTH LEAVECHURCH MOVEOUT
/STATISTICS MEAN VARIANCE RANGE.
```

Results

Table 4.1 Descriptive Measures for YBIRTH, LEAVECHURCH, and MOVEOUT

Descriptive Statistics				
	N	**Range**	**Mean**	**Variance**
ybirth year of birth	1974	52	1952.75	189.002
leavechurch age at which the respondent left church	443	49	23.75	77.802
moveout age at which respondent left parental home	1819	59	21.85	19.517
Valid N (listwise)	426			

Optional Subcommands

The SAVE subcommand saves the z scores of the specified variables on DESCRIPTIVES with new names—that is, the old name preceded by a "Z" by default. A different name can also be specified by placing the new name in parentheses behind the variable name on the first line of the command. The MISSING subcommand determines how the missing or invalid values are treated. If this subcommand is omitted, respondents are only excluded on variables on which they have a missing or invalid value. Respondents are excluded on *all* variables if they have a missing or invalid value on at least one variable using LISTWISE in the MISSING subcommand (see extensive example).

Extensive Example

```
DESCRIPTIVES YBIRTH (Z_YBIRTH) MOVEOUT (Z_MOVEOUT)
/SAVE
/MISSING LISTWISE.
```

In this example, the z scores for YBIRTH and MOVEOUT are saved as Z_YBIRTH and Z_MOVEOUT, respectively. The last line specifies that respondents with a missing or invalid value on one or both variables will not have a z score on *both* variables (Table 4.2).

Results

```
DESCRIPTIVES Z_YBIRTH Z_MOVEOUT.
```

Table 4.2   The z Variables Z_YBIRTH and Z_MOVEOUT With Missing Listwise (n = 1,819)

Descriptive Statistics					
	N	**Minimum**	**Maximum**	**Mean**	**Std. Deviation**
Z_YBIRTH Zscore: year of birth	1819	−2.01275	1.96848	.000	1.000
Z_MOVEOUT Zscore: age at which respondent left parental home	1819	−4.72010	8.63483	.000	1.000
Valid N (listwise)	1819				

4.3 FREQUENCIES △

Function

This command is used to display the frequency distribution. Additionally, statistical measures such as the mean, standard deviation, and percentiles, as well as graphs of frequency distributions can be retrieved.

Structure

The FREQUENCY command is followed by a list of variables to display the desired distributions.

Example

> FREQUENCIES SEX EDUC.

- Results are displayed in Tables 3.11 and 3.14 of Chapter 3.

Optional Subcommands

The FORMAT subcommand can be used to adapt the content of the table. For example, FORMAT is used to change the order in which the values are displayed. AVALUE sorts the values in ascending order (the default setting for FREQUENCY) while DVALUE sorts the values in descending order. AFREQ sorts by increasing frequency (most common value at the last) and DFREQ by decreasing frequency. Additionally, LIMIT followed by a number in parentheses (e.g., 15), specifies that no tables are displayed for variables with more than 15 categories. This is used if one wants to exclude large tables associated with ratio or interval variables. The display of tables can also be avoided by using the NOTABLE subcommand.

The BARCHART, PIECHART, and HISTOGRAM subcommands can be used to display the frequency distributions as a graph. HISTOGRAM can also be complemented by the NORMAL subcommand, which displays the normal distribution in the graph, so that the level of skewness and the peaked nature of the distribution can be assessed.

PERCENTILES can be used to display the percentiles of variables. This subcommand is followed by a number of values between 0 and 100. For example, "/PERCENTILES 25 50 75" calculates the quartiles and the median.

Statistical measures are calculated by SPSS using the STATISTICS subcommand. The same instructions are used for the STATISTICS and DESCRIPTIVES subcommands (p. 73). Additionally, you can calculate the MEDIAN and MODE, as well as statistics on the skewness and peaked nature of the distribution. (See the SPSS help function [p. 16] for more details.)

Finally, the treatment of missing values can be specified using the MISSING subcommand. All missing values are excluded by default. All invalid values (with the exception of absent values or "system missings") are included as valid values with "/MISSING INCLUDE."

Extensive Example

```
FREQUENCIES SEX EDUC
  /FORMAT AFREQ LIMIT(7)
  /BARCHART
  /STATISTICS MINIMUM MAXIMUM MEAN STDDEV
  /MISSING INCLUDE.
```

This example displays the frequency distribution and bar chart for the variables SEX and EDUC. FORMAT indicates that the tables and graphs are to be ordered by frequency and that the table for EDUC is not to be displayed, as this variable exceeds seven categories. STATISTICS displays the highest and lowest values along with the mean and standard deviation. The variable EDUC has a number of missing values, but since these categories may be valuable to see, the last line of the syntax includes these values (Table 4.3, Figure 4.1).

Results

Note: Bar chart for the variable SEX is not displayed.

Table 4.3 Statistical Measures of SEX and EDUC and a Frequency Table of SEX

Statistics		Sex	educ highest completed education
N	Valid	1974	1970
	Missing	0	4
Mean		1.52	4.31
Std. Deviation		.500	2.232
Minimum		1	1
Maximum		2	8

(Continued)

Table 4.3 (Continued)

		Frequency	Percent	Valid Percent	Cumulative Percent
				Sex	
Valid	1 Male	945	47.9	47.9	47.9
	2 Female	1029	52.1	52.1	100.0
	Total	1974	100.0	100.0	

Figure 4.1 Bar Chart for EDUC

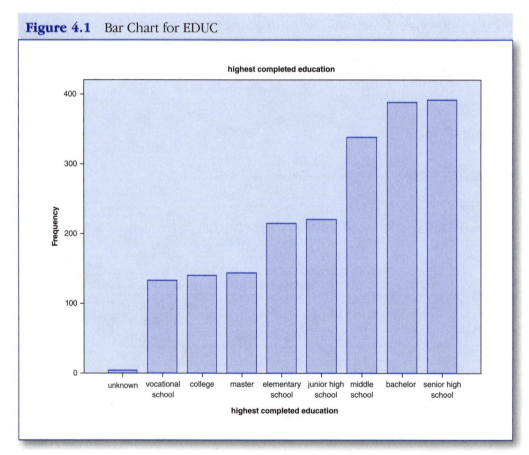

Note: Bar chart for sex not displayed.

4.4 CROSSTABS △

Function

The CROSSTABS command creates cross tables and displays numbers or percentages in its cells. The relationship between variables in the cross table can be examined using a number of correlation measures.

Structure

CROSSTABS is followed by the subcommand BY and the variable names. The first variable in the syntax is displayed in the rows, while the second is displayed in the columns. Adding one or more control variables splits the table by this variable(s) (so-called elaboration). When the causal relationship between the variables is clear, the outcome (y) variable is commonly displayed in the rows (first), the causal (x) variable in the columns (second), and finally, the control variable(s), if applicable. Although more than one control variable can be requested, it is recommended to limit these, as the tables quickly become too large and confusing (Table 4.4a).

Example

CROSSTABS CHRISTP BY CHURCHMEMBER.

Results

Table 4.4a Cross Table CHURCHMEMBER/CHRISTP

christp voting for Christian party * church membership Crosstabulation				
Count				
		Church Membership		
		0 No	1 Yes	Total
christp voting for Christian party	.00 No	876	354	1230
	1.00 Yes	49	331	380
Total		925	685	1610
Note: Only numbers.				

Optional Subcommands

Multiple tables can be displayed with a single CROSSTABS command using extra TABLES subcommands following the first set of variables. In each TABLE, subcommand variables are again separated by the subcommand BY. The default setting for CROSSTABS displays the number of respondents in each cell. You can change this with the CELLS subcommand. Other subcommands can be used to further specify the content of the cells. COUNT displays the number of observations (default); ROW displays the row percentages; COLUMN displays the column percentages; TOTAL presents the cell percentages based on the number of observations; EXPECTED presents the expected number of respondents per cell should you like to determine statistical (in)dependence; RESID presents the difference between the observed and the expected number of respondents in the cell; and ALL displays all possible values and percentages in the cells (not recommended). The STATISTICS subcommand obtains commonly used measures of association: CHISQ is used for a chi-square (χ^2) test; PHI presents Cramér's V; CTAU and BTAU are two variations of Kendall's τ; CORR displays the Pearson's correlation coefficient and the rank-order correlation of Spearman; and RISK presents the odds ratio. You can display the values in the table in ascending (default) or descending order with the FORMAT command followed by the AVALUE or DVALUE subcommands, respectively.

Extensive Example

```
CROSSTABS CHRISTP BY CHURCHMEMBER
/TABLES CHRISTP BY CHURCHMEMBER BY EDUC2
/CELLS COLUMN COUNT EXPECTED
/STATISTICS CHISQ PHI.
```

This syntax will produce two cross tables (Tables 4.4b and c), with the column percentage in each cell (we assume that being a church member causally precedes voting), as well as the absolute and expected number of observations. Furthermore, the chi-square test and Cramér's V are calculated. This is followed by an elaboration: First, the strength and significance of the correlation between church membership and voting for Christian parties are calculated. Second, this association is determined separately for the lower and higher educated. Education does not appear to explain the strong relationship between church membership and voting for Christian parties, because Cramér's V remains virtually unchanged. We would like to note that educational attainment would only have been a plausible explanation if the Cramér's *V* statistic dropped significantly in both cases.

Results

Table 4.4b   Cross Tables CHURCHMEMBER/CHRIST

Crosstab					
			churchmember		
			0 No	**1 Yes**	**Total**
christp voting for Christian party	.00 No	Count	876	354	1230
		Expected count	706.7	523.3	1230.0
		Within churchmember (%)	94.7	51.7	76.4
	1.00 Yes	Count	49	331	380
		Expected count	218.3	161.7	380.0
		Within churchmember (%)	5.3	48.3	23.6
Total		Count	925	685	1610
		Expected count	925.0	685.0	1610.0
		Within churchmember (%)	100.0	100.0	100.0

Note: With column percentages, absolute numbers, and expected numbers.

Table 4.4c   Chi-Square Test and Cramér's *V*: Bivariate Relationship and Controlled for Education in Two Categories (EDUC2)

Chi-Square Tests					
	Value	**df**	**Asymp. Sig. (2-Sided)**	**Exact Sig. (2-Sided)**	**Exact Sig. (1-Sided)**
Pearson chi-square	404.007[a]	1	.000		
Continuity correction[b]	401.624	1	.000		
Likelihood ratio	427.465	1	.000		
Fishers exact test				.000	.000
Linear-by-linear association	403.756	1	.000		
N of valid cases	1610				

Note: a. Zero cells (0%) have expected count less than 5. The minimum expected count is 161.68.

b. Computed only for a 2 × 2 table.

(Continued)

Table 4.4c (Continued)

Symmetric Measures		Value	Approx. Sig.
Nominal by nominal	Phi	.501	.000
	Cramer's V	.501	.000
N of valid cases		1610	

Symmetric Measures				
educ2 education in two categories			Value	Approx. Sig.
1.00 low	Nominal by nominal	Phi	.504	.000
		Cramer's V	.504	.000
	N of valid cases		909	
2.00 high	Nominal by nominal	Phi	.496	.000
		Cramer's V	.496	.000
	N of valid cases		698	
Total	Nominal by nominal	Phi	.501	.000
		Cramer's V	.501	.000
	N of valid cases		1607	

△ 4.5 EXAMINE

Function

The EXAMINE command numerically and graphically examines the distribution of a variable with ordinal measurement levels or higher.

Structure

The EXAMINE command is followed by a list of variables. This is followed by the PLOT, BOXPLOT, or STEMLEAF subcommands to display these graphical representations (Table 4.5, Figure 4.2).

Example

```
EXAMINE YBIRTH
  /PLOT BOXPLOT.
```

Results

Table 4.5 Numeric Representation of YBIRTH

Descriptives				Statistic	Std. Error
ybirth year of birth	Mean			1952.75	.309
	95% Confidence interval of mean	Lower bound		1952.14	
		Upper bound		1953.35	
	5% Trimmed mean			1952.96	
	Median			1954.00	
	Variance			189.002	
	Std. Deviation			13.748	
	Minimum			1925	
	Maximum			1977	
	Range			52	
	Interquartile range			21	
	Skewness			−.237	.055
	Kurtosis			−.922	.110

Figure 4.2   Graphic Representation of YBIRTH

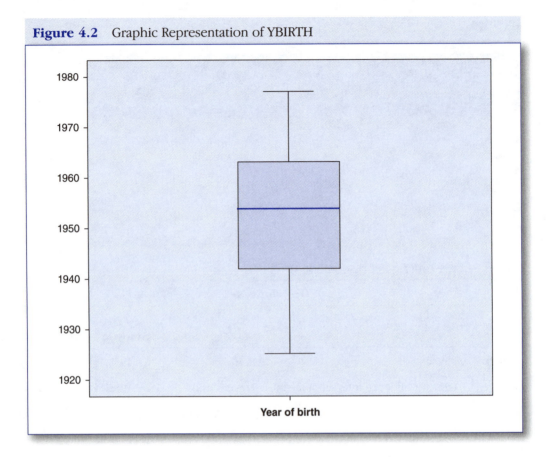

△ 4.6 GRAPH

Function

GRAPH is used to produce a variety of graphs and plots such as bar charts, pie charts, and scatterplots. It is more convenient to specify these through the menu, because the syntax for this command is very extensive, and there are a lot of different graphs, with numerous subtypes. An example of how to create a syntax with "paste" for a diagram plotting the mean of church members against education is given below.

- Select the data or syntax window GRAPH → Legacy Dialogs → Line . . .
- Then, select Define.

- Check under "Line Represents" *Other* statistic (e.g., mean) (see Figure 4.3a).
- Place CHURCHMEMBER in the box below Variable and the variable EDUC under Category Axis (see Figure 4.3a) by selecting the variable and then checking the arrow (▶).
- "Paste" the command if identical to Figure 4.3a.

Figure 4.3a   Dialogue Box "Define Simple Line"

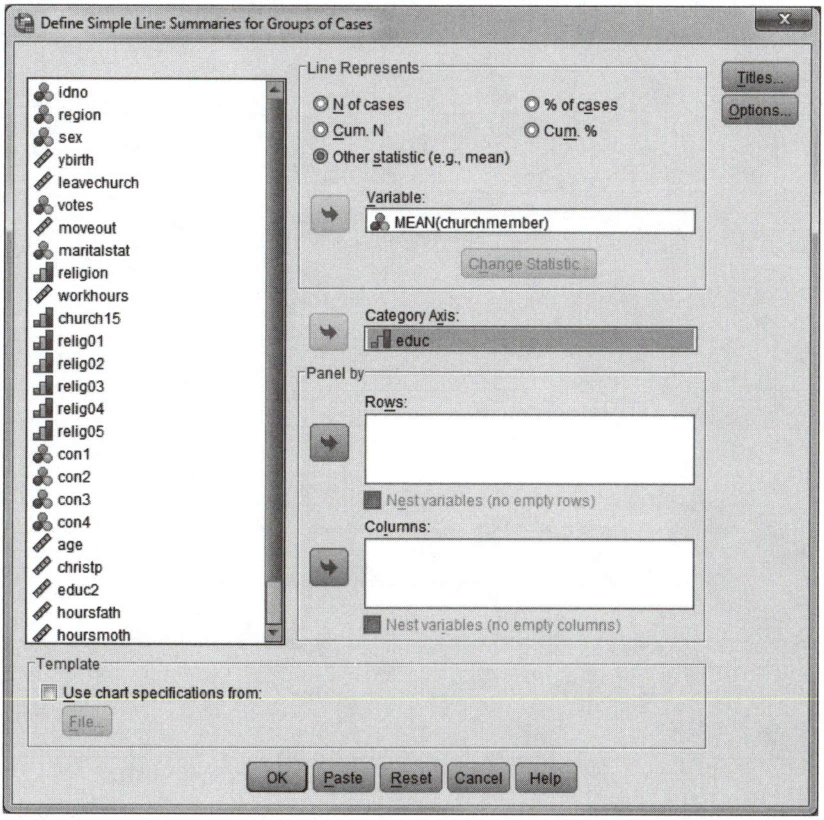

The syntax window will display the following syntax:
GRAPH
/LINE(SIMPLE)=MEAN (churchmember) BY educ.

Executing this command produces a diagram of the mean of church membership for each category of education. Since church membership only has values 0 (no) and 1 (yes), this is equal to the proportion of church members for each category of education (see Figure 4.3b).

Figure 4.3b Proportion of Church Members for Each Educational Category

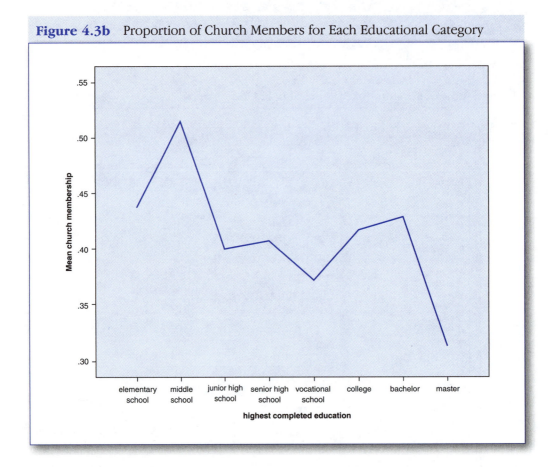

△ 4.7 MEANS

Function

The MEANS command is used to show means and other statistical measurements of interval/ratio variables per category or group. It is also possible to test the differences globally for significance. (See T-TEST on p. 90 for an extensive method to compare groups.)

Structure

The MEANS command is followed by the variable(s) from which you want the statistical information, followed by the subcommand BY, which specifies the variable distinguishing the categories or groups. This command can further be followed by multiple BY subcommands to show information from the groups that represent each combination of categories from multiple variables.

Example

> MEANS YBIRTH BY SEX BY REGION.

In this example, the means, number of cases, and standard deviations of YBIRTH are calculated, for the combination of SEX and REGION. This results in eight distinct groups, since there are men and women from four regions (see Table 4.6a).

Optional Subcommands

The MEANS default setting produces means, number of observations, and standard deviations for each group. This is adapted by using the CELLS subcommand, followed by a list of instructions, such as MEAN (mean), STDDEV (standard deviation), COUNT (number of cases), MEDIAN (median), MIN (minimum), MAX (maximum), VARIANCE (variance), or ALL (all of the above, plus some less common statistical measurements). (See the SPSS help function [p. 16] for a complete list.)

The subcommand STATISTICS performs an analysis of variance (ANOVA) and/or a linearity test (LINEARITY). These terms will follow the STATISTICS subcommand. Using only LINEARITY also displays ANOVA results (see the example below).

Extensive Example

> MEANS RELIGION BY EDUC
> /CELLS MEAN MIN MAX
> /STATISTICS LINEARITY.

Table 4.6a Mean of YBIRTH for Each Combination of SEX/REGION and Per REGION

| | | ybirth year of birth | | |
| | region Region where the respondent was | | | |
Sex	interviewed	Mean	N	Std. Deviation
1 Male	1 North	1951.02	95	14.341
	2 East	1953.20	213	13.550
	3 West	1952.39	429	13.719
	4 South	1952.15	208	14.282
	Total	1952.38	945	13.861
2 Female	1 North	1951.95	122	13.395
	2 East	1952.97	228	14.151
	3 West	1953.46	462	13.492
	4 South	1953.02	217	13.605
	Total	1953.08	1029	13.641
Total	1 North	1951.54	217	13.792
	2 East	1953.08	441	13.849
	3 West	1952.95	891	13.605
	4 South	1952.60	425	13.931
	Total	1952.75	1974	13.748

This syntax produces the mean, minimum, and maximum values of the variable RELIGION for each category of the variable EDUC (Table 4.6a). Linearity is calculated and an ANOVA test is performed (Table 4.6b), including measures of association Pearson's r and eta (Table 4.6c).

Results

Table 4.6b Means and ANOVA Tables

Report			
religion degree of religiousness (low score = not religious)			
educ highest completed education	**Mean**	**Minimum**	**Maximum**
1 Middle school	2.0382	.00	4.00
2 Junior high school	1.9026	.00	4.00
3 Senior high school	1.7521	.00	4.00
4 Vocational school	1.6259	.00	4.00
5 College	1.3809	.00	3.80
6 Bachelor degrees	1.5493	.00	4.00
7 Master degrees	1.5457	.00	4.00
8	1.3176	.00	4.00
Total	1.6670	.00	4.00

ANOVA Table							
			Sum of Squares	df	Mean Square	F	Sig.
religion degree of religiousness (low score=not religious) * **educ** highest completed education	Between groups	(Combined)	80.895	7	11.556	10.587	.000
		Linearity	65.715	1	65.715	60.205	.000
		Deviation from linearity	15.180	6	2.530	2.318	.031
	Within groups		2029.129	1859	1.092		
	Total		2110.023	1866			

Table 4.6c Correlation (*R*) and Eta for EDUC/RELIGION

Measures of Association				
	R	**R Squared**	**Eta**	**Eta Squared**
religion degree of religiousness (low score = not religious) * **educ** highest completed education	−.176	.031	.196	.038

△ 4.8 T-TEST

Function

The T-TEST command tests whether two means are significantly different from each other. You can use it to test whether a sample mean differs from a hypothesized population mean or to test whether the means in two groups differ. These groups can be independent (e.g., a group of randomly selected men and a group of randomly selected women) or dependent (e.g., the same group with means on two comparable variables).

Structure

To test a mean against an assumed (hypothetical) value, the subcommand TESTVAL with the hypothesized mean value follows T-TEST, followed by the VARIABLES subcommand and one or more variables whose mean has to be tested (see Example 1).

To test group means in two independent groups, the GROUPS subcommand and the variable names follow the T-TEST command. Parentheses are placed around the groups that are to be compared, followed by the VARIABLES subcommand and the names of the variables to be tested (see Example 2).

The PAIRS subcommand follows the T-TEST command to compare the means of two dependent groups, followed by the two variables you want to compare (see Example 3).

Examples

Example 1: Tests the hypothesis that the average age of the respondents in the sample differs significantly from 40 (Table 4.7a):

```
T-TEST TESTVAL 40
  /VARIABLES AGE.
```

Example 2 (independent groups): Tests whether the average age of married respondents differs from divorced respondents. The values 2 and 3 that follow MARITALSTAT are the values that refer to the categories "Married" and "Divorced" (Table 4.7b):

```
T-TEST GROUPS MARITALSTAT (2 3)
  /VARIABLES AGE.
```

Example 3 (dependent groups): Tests whether the mean number of hours of labor for employed sons is significantly different than that of their employed fathers (Table 4.7c).

```
T-TEST PAIRS HOURSSON HOURSFATH.
```

Results

Table 4.7a   T-Test for AGE (Test Value in Null Hypothesis [H0] = 40)

One-Sample Statistics				
	N	Mean	Std. Deviation	Std. Error Mean
age	1974	42.2533	13.74781	.30943

One-Sample Test						
Test Value = 40						
					95% Confidence Interval of the Difference	
	t	df	Sig. (two-tailed)	Mean Difference	Lower	Upper
Age	7.282	1973	.000	2.25329	1.6465	2.8601

Table 4.7b   T-Test for AGE (Married vs. Divorced)

Group Statistics					
	maritalstat marital status	N	Mean	Std. Deviation	Std. Error Mean
age	2 Married	1223	45.7441	11.75573	.33615
	3 Divorced	125	47.7440	9.65444	.86352

(Continued)

Table 4.7b (Continued)

		Levene's Test for Equality of Variances		T-Test for Equality of Means					
		F	**Sig.**	**T**	**df**	**Sig. (two-tailed)**	**Mean Difference**	**Std. Error Difference**
age	Equal variances assumed	12.75	.000	−1.840	1346	.066	−1.99993	1.08721
	Equal variances not assumed			−2.158	164.04	.032	−1.99993	.92664

Table 4.7c T-Test for Labor Hours (Sons vs. Fathers)

Paired Samples Correlations			
	N	**Correlation**	**Sig.**
hoursson hours of labor of son & **hoursfath** hours of labor of father respondent	861	.191	.000

Paired Samples Test								
	Paired Differences							
				95% Confidence Interval of the Difference				**Sig. (two-tailed)**
	Mean	**Std. Dev.**	**Std. Error**	**Lower**	**Upper**	**t**	**df**	
hoursson hours of labor of son − **hoursfath** hours of labor of father respondent	−6.532	15.27	.5205	−7.554	−5.510	−12.5	860	.000

4.9 CORRELATIONS △

Function

The CORRELATIONS command calculates the Pearson's correlation coefficient and statistical probabilities (*p* values).

Structure

The CORRELATIONS command is followed by a list of variables to calculate the correlations between these variables.

Example

CORRELATIONS LEAVECHURCH MOVEOUT.

This example calculates the correlation between the age at which the respondents became disaffiliated and the age at which the respondents left their parental home (Table 4.8a).

Results

Table 4.8a   Correlation Between CHURCHMEMBER and MOVEOUT

Correlations		leavechurch age at which the respondent left church	moveout age at which the respondent left parental home
leavechurch age at which the respondent left church	Pearson correlation	1	.211
	Sig. (two-tailed)		.000
	N	443	426
moveout age at which the respondent left parental home	Pearson correlation	.211	1
	Sig. (two-tailed)	.000	
	N	426	1819

Optional Subcommands

The MISSING subcommand specifies how missing values are treated. PAIRWISE calculates the correlation for respondents with valid scores on both variables. LISTWISE calculates the correlation only for respondents with valid scores on every variable listed.

The PRINT subcommand specifies a one- or two-tailed significance test. The default setting uses a two-tailed test. ONETAIL following the PRINT subcommand uses a one-tailed significance test.

Extensive Example

```
CORRELATIONS WORKHOURS HOURSFATH HOURSMOTH
/MISSING PAIRWISE
/PRINT ONETAIL.
```

In this example, the correlations are calculated between the working hours of employed respondents, their employed fathers, and employed mothers. Each correlation uses the maximum number of respondents (pairwise), and one-tailed significance levels are presented (Table 4.8b).

Results

Table 4.8b Pearson Correlations Between WORKHOURS, HOURSFATH, and HOURSMOTH

Correlations		*workhours* hours of labor in a week	*hoursfath* hours of labor of father respondent	*hoursmoth* hours of labor of mother
workhours hours of labor in a week	Pearson correlation	1	.123	.163
	Sig. (one-tailed)		.000	.001
	N	1824	1743	345
hoursfath hours of labor of father respondent	Pearson correlation	.123	1	.379
	Sig. (one-tailed)	.000		.000
	N	1743	1885	380
hoursmoth hours of labor of mother	Pearson Correlation	.163	.379	1
	Sig. (one-tailed)	.001	.000	
	N	345	380	397

4.10 REGRESSION △

Function

The REGRESSION command is used to perform (multiple) linear regression analysis. This command also features a number of extra options, including residual plots and tests for collinearity. Some important options are discussed in the following section.

Structure

The REGRESSION command is followed by the DEPENDENT subcommand and the name of the dependent variable (y). This is followed by the METHOD and ENTER subcommands, and the names of the independent variables (x).

Example

```
REGRESSION
/DEPENDENT RELIGION
/METHOD ENTER AGE EDUC3 SEX.
```

In this example, a linear regression model is used with the (factor) scores (p. 107) on RELIGION as dependent variable, and AGE, EDUC3, and SEX as predictor variables (Table 4.9a).

Results

Note: Only the most important results are shown.

Table 4.9a   RELIGION Explained by AGE, EDUC2, and SEX

	Coefficients[a]				
	Unstandardized Coefficients		Standardized Coefficients		
Model	B	Std. Error	Beta	t	Sig.
(Constant)	1.279	.156		8.192	.000
Age	.016	.002	.205	9.072	.000
Educ3 education in years	−.042	.008	−.122	−5.376	.000
Sex	.150	.048	.071	3.131	.002
Note: a. Dependent variable: religion. Degree of religiousness (low score = not religious)					

Optional Subcommands

In this section's first example, the subcommand METHOD was followed by the ENTER instruction to include the independent variables. This specifies that all variables must be included in the model. It is also possible to examine the significance of the model for each variable step by step, so that the most parsimonious model can be obtained. For this, ENTER is replaced by BACKWARD, FORWARD, or STEPWISE (mostly used) as a selection method. As with the ENTER instruction, these instructions are also followed by a list of variables. The CRITERIA subcommand specifies the criteria for which a variable is considered significant. The subcommand is followed by specifying PIN (= the maximum probability that leads to including the variable) and POUT (= the maximum probability that does not lead to excluding the variable) values. The default setting (if CRITERIA is not used) is .05 for PIN and .10 for POUT. This means that effects with a p value equal to or lower than .05 are included in the model and effects with a p value higher than .10 are excluded from the model. Please notice that for a one-tailed significance test with alpha (α) = .05, the PIN is set too low! In this case, we recommend the criteria of PIN = .10 and POUT = .20.

The STATISTICS subcommand displays a number of statistical measurements. When this is not specified, SPSS presents a table with the (multiple) correlation coefficient (R), the explained variance (R^2), and the adjusted variance (adjusted R^2). You can also calculate this by using the R instruction following STATISTICS. By default, SPSS also presents a table with results for the variance analysis (*instruction:* ANOVA) and a table with the coefficients of the regression equation (*instruction:* COEFF). Other useful options include COLLIN for information on collinearity and CI for confidence intervals of the coefficients.

Outliers can be identified using the RESIDUALS subcommand followed by the OUTLIERS subcommand. A list of (temporary) variables follows OUTLIERS, indicating which type of outliers should be displayed. You can select RESID (residuals), ZRESID (standardized residuals), SDRESID (studentized deleted residuals), MAHAL (Mahalanobis distance), COOK (Cook's distance), and LEVER (leverage values).

The SAVE subcommand permanently saves the temporary variables in the (active) data file: The subcommand is followed by the names of the temporary variables that will be saved. Inserting a new name in parentheses following the temporary name changes the name of the temporary variables. If new names are not specified, the temporary names will be used in the data set.

The SCATTERPLOT subcommand displays a scatterplot of the temporary variables and is followed by the name of two variables between parentheses (Figure 4.4). These are indicated by placing an asterisk (*) before the variable. The predicted values are named PRED; hence that name should be used here. A scatterplot with the predicted values (*PRED) against the standardized residuals (*ZRESID) is specified to check whether the assumptions of linearity and homoscedasticity are met. The sequence of the subcommands is important for the REGRES-SION command. For the command to be executed, all subcommands have to be in the prescribed order. The correct sequence is STATISTICS, CRITERIA, DEPENDENT, METHOD, RESIDUALS, SAVE, and finally SCAT-TERPLOT.

We have only mentioned some of the possible options used with the REGRESSION command. For other options, see the menu (Analyze → Regression → Linear), SPSS's help function (p. 16), or the PDF file (p. 16).

Extensive Example

```
REGRESSION
 /STATISTICS R ANOVA COEFF COLLIN
 /CRITERIA PIN(.10) POUT(.20)
 /DEPENDENT RELIGION
 /METHOD STEPWISE SEX EDUC3 AGE
 WORKHOURS
 /RESIDUALS OUTLIERS(SDRESID, MAHAL, COOK)
 /SAVE PRED (PREDICT)
 /SCATTERPLOT (*ZRESID, *PRED).
DESCRIPTIVES PREDICT.
```

In this example, religion is the outcome (dependent) variable and is predicted (explained) by SEX, EDUC3, AGE, and WORKHOURS. STEPWISE is used instead of ENTER, so SPSS uses a selection procedure to determine which variables to include in the model. The CRITERIA subcommand specifies the requirements of each variable included in the model: a probability lesser than or equal to .10 includes a variable, whereas a probability greater than .20 excludes a variable from the model (Table 4.9b).

Information regarding the validity of the model can also be retrieved. Here indicators on collinearity (COLLIN) are calculated, as well as possible outliers associated with SDRESID, MAHAL, and COOK. A scatterplot is also drawn in which the predicted values are plotted against the residuals. Finally, with SAVE, the predicted values are saved as PREDICT, and the mean of this variable is calculated with DESCRIPTIVES (see Tables 4.9c/d and Figure 4.4).

Results

Note: Only the most important tables have been selected.

Table 4.9b Explained Variance per Model, Effect Estimates, and Collinearity Diagnostics

Model	R	R Square	Adjusted R Square	Std. Error of the Estimate
1	.220	.048	.048	1.03786
2	.256	.065	.064	1.02877
3	.265	.070	.068	1.02650

Model		Unstandardized Coefficients		Standardized Coefficients	t	Sig.
		B	Std. Error	Beta		
1	(Constant)	.896	.086		10.362	.000
	Age	.018	.002	.220	9.343	.000
2	(Constant)	1.518	.140		10.836	.000
	Age	.016	.002	.200	8.458	.000
	educ3 education in years	−.045	.008	−.132	−5.615	.000
3	(Constant)	1.244	.168		7.396	.000
	Age	.017	.002	.204	8.644	.000
	educ3 education in years	−.042	.008	−.124	−5.215	.000
	Sex	.147	.050	.069	2.933	.003

				Variance Proportions			
Model	**Dim.**	**Eigenvalue**	**Condition Index**	**(Constant)**	**age**	**educ3**	**Sex**
1	1	1.957	1.000	.02	.02		
	2	.043	6.765	.98	.98		
2	1	2.895	1.000	.00	.01	.01	
	2	.084	5.863	.00	.54	.31	
	3	.021	11.866	.99	.45	.68	
3	1	3.805	1.000	.00	.01	.00	.01
	2	.096	6.304	.00	.25	.03	.66
	3	.083	6.756	.00	.38	.39	.06
	4	.016	15.505	1.00	.37	.58	.28

Collinearity Diagnostics[a]

Note: a. Dependent Variable: religion. Degree of religiousness (low score = not religious).

Table 4.9c Collinearity Diagnostics and Residuals

Outlier Statistics[a]

		Case Number	**Statistic**	**Sig. F**
Stud. deleted residual	1	765	2.735	
	2	313	2.725	
	3	1828	2.505	
	4	1571	2.500	
	5	418	2.497	
	6	902	2.461	
	7	707	2.443	
	8	691	2.425	
	9	564	2.414	
	10	399	2.370	
Mahalanobis distance	1	39	10.675	
	2	724	9.357	
	3	626	9.308	

(Continued)

Table 4.9c (Continued)

Outlier Statistics[a]		Case Number	Statistic	Sig. F
	4	31	9.301	
	5	324	9.014	
	6	1573	8.967	
	7	1081	8.967	
	8	690	8.967	
	9	1846	8.732	
	10	97	8.508	
Cook's distance	1	1659	.007	1.000
	2	340	.007	1.000
	3	313	.006	1.000
	4	1099	.006	1.000
	5	845	.006	1.000
	6	902	.006	1.000
	7	1828	.006	1.000
	8	799	.006	1.000
	9	339	.006	1.000
	10	765	.006	1.000

Note: a. Dependent Variable: religion. Degree of religiousness (low score = not religious).

Table 4.9d Scatter Mean, Minimum and Maximum, and Standard Deviation of PREDICT

	N	Minimum	Maximum	Mean	Std. Deviation
PREDICT Unstandardized predicted value	1970	1.11114	2.44631	1.6605	.291178
Valid N (listwise)	1970				

Figure 4.4 Scatterplot of Residuals Against Predicted Values of PREDICT

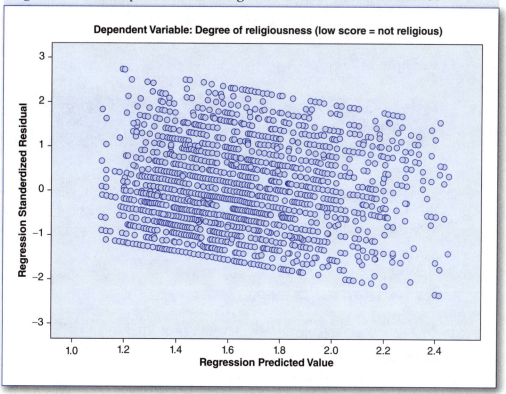

Dependent Variable: Degree of religiousness (low score = not religious)

4.11 LOGISTIC REGRESSION[1] △

Function

The command LOGISTIC REGRESSION is used to perform a logistic regression (applicable if the dependent variable is dichotomous).

Structure

The LOGISTIC REGRESSION command is followed by the name of the dependent variable, the METHOD and ENTER subcommands, and finally the names of the independent variables.

---

[1]This procedure may not be available in every SPSS license—the Regression Module of Advanced Statistics has to be installed.

The dependent variable is dichotomous, meaning that there are only two valid values. In principal, these are 0 and 1, but if this is not the case, SPSS will recode them into 0 and 1.

Example

> LOGISTIC REGRESSION CHURCHMEMBER
> /METHOD ENTER AGE SEX.

In this example, CHURCHMEMBER (0 = not a member, 1 = member) is the dependent variable, and AGE and SEX are the independent variables (predictors) (Table 4.10a).

Results

Note: Only the most important tables have been selected.

Table 4.10a Logistic Regression With CHURCHMEMBER as Dependent Variable and AGE and SEX as Predictors

Omnibus Tests of Model Coefficients		Chi-Square	df	Sig.
Step 1	Step	66.319	2	.000
	Block	66.319	2	.000
	Model	66.319	2	.000

Model Summary			
	−2 Log likelihood	Cox and Snell R Square	Nagelkerke R Square
Step 1	2559.852	.034	.045

Variables in the Equation	B	S.E.	Wald	df	Sig.	Exp(B)
Age	.026	.003	58.105	1	.000	1.027
Sex	.262	.094	7.734	1	.005	1.299
Constant	−1.829	.217	70.998	1	.000	.161

Optional Subcommands

The CONTRAST subcommand specifies the variables that are to be included as dummy variables (a dummy variable is a dichotomous variable, coded 0 and 1). The command is followed by the variable (between brackets) followed by the required contrast (*options*: INDICATOR [most common], SIMPLE, DEVIATION, DIFFERENCE, HELMERT, REPEATED, POLYNOMIAL, SPECIAL), often followed by a reference category (as a number). We refer you to SPSS help files for more information on the contrast options (check help → menu → topics, and then type the word *contrasts* as keyword and double-click "in Logistic Regression" from the list.

BSTEP (starting with a full model) and FSTEP (starting with an empty model) can also be used; they follow the METHOD command. PIN and POUT values can be adapted with these selection methods (see p. 96 for an explanation of PIN/POUT). Default values are .05 and .10. These values can be changed when using the CRITERIA subcommand.

SAVE allows you to save the predicted scores (PRED) to the active data file.

Extensive Example

```
LOGISTIC REGRESSION CHURCHMEMBER
 /CONTRAST (CHURCH15) = INDICATOR(1)
 /CONTRAST (EDUC) = INDICATOR(3)
 /METHOD = BSTEP AGE SEX CHURCH15 EDUC
 /CRITERIA = PIN(.10) POUT(.20) ITERATE(20) CUT(.5)
 /SAVE = PRED(PRED) .
GRAPH LINE=MEAN(PRED) by EDUC.
```

In this example, CHURCHMEMBER is the dependent variable. Visiting the church at the age of 15 (CHURCH15) and the highest completed education (EDUC) are ordinal variables and should be included as dummy variables, where "once a week" (first category) and "junior high school" (third category, just used to illustrate that any category may serve as a reference) are specified as the reference category (Tables 4.10b and c). The model starts with all variables and removes variables without significant effects. Finally, the predicted scores are saved and plotted against educational attainment (Figure 4.5a).

Results

Note: Only the most important tables have been selected.

Table 4.10b Logistic Regression of CHURCHMEMBER on AGE, SEX, and CHURCH15 and EDUC (Categorical or Dummified): Effects

		B	S.E.	Wald	df	Sig.	Exp(B)
				Variables in the Equation			
Step 1[a]	Age	.006	.005	1.356	1	.244	1.006
	Sex	.274	.129	4.506	1	.034	1.315
	church15			475.813	4	.000	
	church15(1)	−.017	.211	.006	1	.937	.983
	church15(2)	−.711	.195	13.267	1	.000	.491
	church15(3)	−2.570	.212	147.279	1	.000	.077
	church15(4)	2.889	.192	227.401	1	.000	17.974
	Educ			24.831	7	.001	
	educ(1)	.100	.284	.124	1	.725	1.105
	educ(2)	.662	.254	6.764	1	.009	1.938
	educ(3)	.205	.250	.674	1	.412	1.227
	educ(4)	.766	.319	5.773	1	.016	2.151
	educ(5)	.550	.315	3.039	1	.081	1.733
	educ(6)	.198	.246	.649	1	.421	1.219
	educ(7)	−.516	.325	2.524	1	.112	.597
	Constant	−1.304	.396	10.869	1	.001	.271
Step 2[a]	sex	.263	.129	4.173	1	.041	1.301
	church15			493.349	4	.000	
	church15(1)	−.049	.209	.054	1	.816	.952
	church15(2)	−.757	.191	15.679	1	.000	.469
	church15(3)	−2.598	.210	152.364	1	.000	.074
	church15(4)	2.899	.191	229.263	1	.000	18.157
	educ			24.189	7	.001	
	educ(1)	.147	.280	.275	1	.600	1.158
	educ(2)	.668	.254	6.909	1	.009	1.950
	educ(3)	.186	.249	.556	1	.456	1.204
	educ(4)	.708	.315	5.057	1	.025	2.030
	educ(5)	.518	.314	2.720	1	.099	1.678
	educ(6)	.193	.246	.616	1	.432	1.213
	educ(7)	−.529	.324	2.665	1	.103	.589
	Constant	−1.009	.302	11.128	1	.001	.365

Note: a. Variable(s) entered on Step 1: age, sex, church15, educ.

Table 4.10c Logistic Regression on CHURCHMEMBER: Log Likelihood and Significance of the Excluded Variable AGE

		Model If Term Removed			
Variable		Model Log Likelihood	Change in −2 Log Likelihood	df	Sig. of the Change
Step 1	age	−787.554	1.355	1	.244
	sex	−789.140	4.528	1	.033
	church15	−1271.996	970.239	4	.000
	educ	−799.867	25.982	7	.001
Step 2	sex	−789.649	4.191	1	.041
	church15	−1299.427	1023.747	4	.000
	educ	−800.217	25.328	7	.001

		Variables Not in the Equation			
			Score	df	Sig.
Step 2	Variables	age	1.358	1	.244
	Overall statistics		1.358	1	.244

Figure 4.5a Mean Estimated Chance to Be a Church Member for Each Category of Education (EDUC)

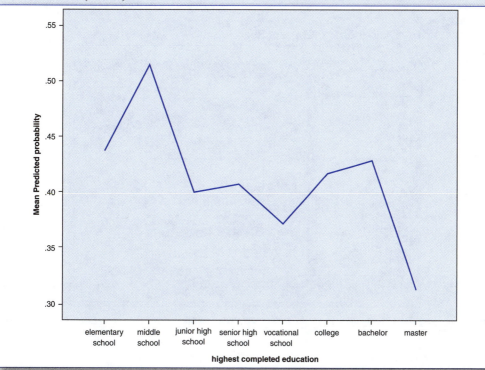

Extensive Example With Use of "Paste"

Since there are a lot of options with logistic regression analysis, we will now demonstrate how to create the syntax from the extensive example with the "paste" option.

- Choose from the data or syntax window Analyze → Regression → Binary Logistic . . .
- Then, check CHURCHMEMBER and place it with ▶ in the box "Dependent" (see Figure 4.5b).
- Then, check AGE and place it in the box "Covariates" (again, see Figure 4.5b) and do the same for SEX, CHURCH15, and EDUC.
- Choose the method for Backward: conditional (Figure 4.5b).
- Choose "Categorical" and check CHURCH15, and place it in the box "Categorical Covariates" and do the same for EDUC (see Figure 4.5c).
- Then, check "Continue" (in the window that appears now, after the variables CHURCH15 and EDUC, it reads (Cat)).
- Check "save" and then "Probabilities." Check "Continue."
- Now, press "Paste."

Figure 4.5b Dialogue Box "Logistic Regression"

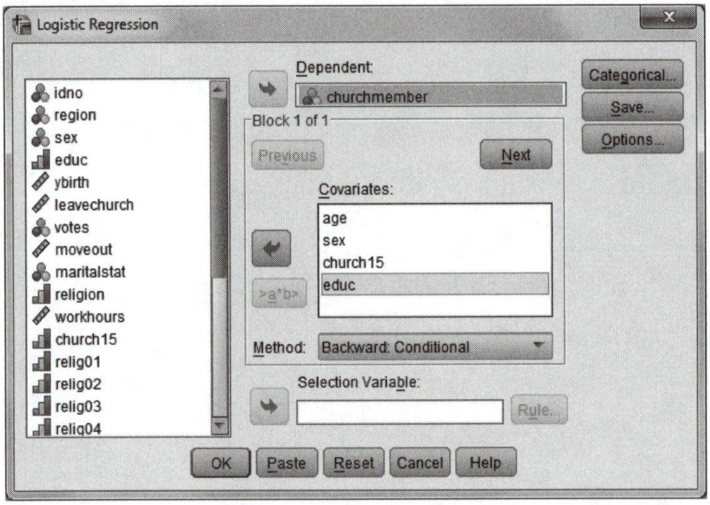

Figure 4.5c   Dialogue Box "Define Categorical Variables"

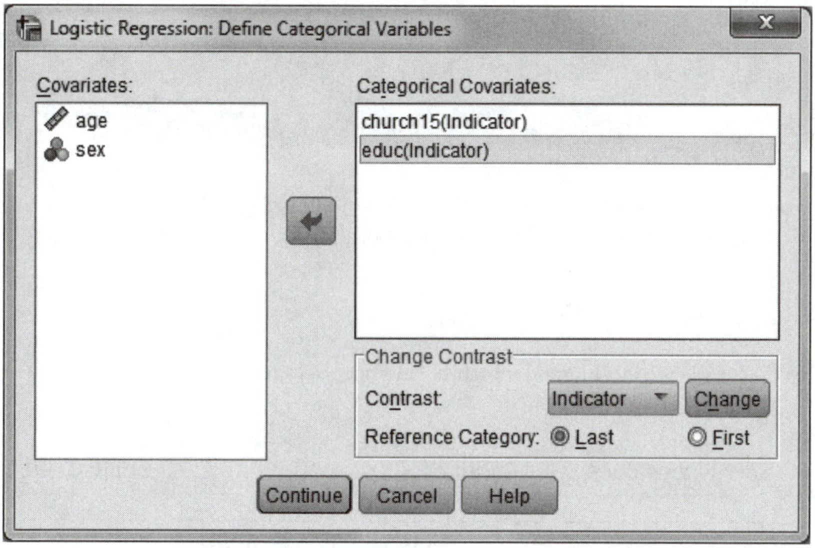

At the bottom of the (active) syntax file, you will find the same syntax as on page 103; the only difference is that the reference category will be displayed as the last category (since SPSS 15). This can be changed by typing "(church15)=indicator (**1**) CONTRAST (educ) =Indicator (**3**)," so that the first and third categories are the reference categories. Executing the syntax will create the same output as in Tables 4.10b and c.

4.12 FACTOR △

Function

The FACTOR command is used to perform principal factor and component analyses (PFA, PCA).

Structure

The command is followed by the subcommand VARIABLES and the variables to be analyzed.

Example

```
FACTOR
 /VARIABLES RELIG01 TO RELIG05.
```

In this example, a principal component analysis is performed on the variables RELIG01 to RELIG05 (Table 4.11a).

Results

Note: Only the most important tables have been selected.

Table 4.11a Eigenvalues and Loadings of Component Analysis RELIG01–RELIG05

	Total Variance Explained					
	Initial Eigenvalues			Extraction Sums of Squared Loadings		
Component	Total	Variance (%)	Cumulative (%)	Total	Variance (%)	Cumulative (%)
1	3.311	66.212	66.212	3.311	66.212	66.212
2	.659	13.189	79.401			
3	.504	10.089	89.490			
4	.338	6.759	96.249			
5	.188	3.751	100.000			

Note: Extraction method: Principal component analysis.

Component Matrix[a]	
	Component
	1
relig01 GOD IS CONCERNED WITH EVERY INDIVIDUAL PERSONALLY	.861
relig02 GOD WANTS TO BE OUR GOD	.891
relig03 LIFE HAS A MEANING BECAUSE OF THE EXISTENCE GOD	.847
relig04 BELIEF IN GOD CAN HELP US BEAR A LOT OF PAIN	.699
relig05 DEATH HAS A MEANING IF YOU BELIEVE IN GOD	.754

Note: Extraction method: Principal component analysis.

a. 1 components extracted.

Optional Subcommands

The FORMAT subcommand is used to specify the output. The instructions FORMAT SORT will sort the variables on their loadings. The BLANK command prevents loadings below a certain value from displaying, which can make the output clearer—you can specify the threshold loading in parentheses after BLANK.

The CRITERIA subcommand can be used to specify certain conditions for the solution. For example, you can specify the number of factors with FACTORS followed by the number in parentheses. The minimum eigenvalue of a factor can be specified with MINEIGEN followed by the value in parentheses. EXTRACTION is used to indicate the model of analysis. If a type of analysis is not specified, SPSS uses default component analysis. When PAF is indicated in the EXTRACTION subcommand, then principal factor analysis is used. In general, this is preferable to component analysis, because component analysis assumes no measurement error, which is a rather strong assumption in social science research.

The ROTATION subcommand refers to the rotation of a solution. SPSS does not rotate without this command. Without specification, SPSS will use a VARIMAX rotation by default if ROTATION is used (this assumes uncorrelated factors). Adding OBLIMIN to ROTATION allows correlations between factors. We recommend starting with OBLIMIN rotation. VARIMAX commonly is used if OBLIMIN shows low correlations between factors. The factor loadings can be saved with SAVE, followed by the method of estimation (the least squares method "REG" is the default option and is commonly used), and is closed with ALL in parentheses. Please note that the subcommands need to be in the exact order mentioned above.

Extensive Example

```
FACTOR
 /VARIABLES RELIG01 TO RELIG05 CON1 TO CON4
 /FORMAT SORT BLANK(.40)
 /CRITERIA FACTORS(2)
 /EXTRACTION PAF
 /ROTATION OBLIMIN
 /SAVE REG (ALL).
DESCRIPTIVES FAC1_1 FAC2_1.
```

In this example, a factor analysis is performed on five variables assumed to measure the degree of religiosity and four variables that capture the degree of (cultural) conservatism. The loadings are sorted and excluded if they fall between .40 and −.40. The analysis is fixed at two factors, and principal factor analysis (PAF) is used as opposed to component analysis. The solution is rotated, and correlations between factors are allowed (OBLIMIN). The scores are saved as FAC1_1 and FAC2_1 and are requested with DESCRIPTIVES (Table 4.11b). We advise calculating the correlations between the factors and the corresponding items to clarify whether a high- or a low-factor score relates to strong religiosity and strong conservatism.

Results

Note: Only the most important tables have been selected.

Table 4.11b Eigenvalues, Factor Loadings, Correlations Between Factors, and Factor Scores of Factor Analysis on RELIG01–05 and CON1–4

Factor	Intial Eigenvalues			Extraction Sums of Squared Loadings			Rotation
	Total	Variance (%)	Cumulative (%)	Total	Variance (%)	Cumulative (%)	Total
1	3.732	41.468	41.468	3.319	36.876	36.876	3.172
2	1.730	19.228	60.696	1.214	13.493	50.369	1.974
3	.771	8.567	69.262				
4	.686	7.623	76.885				
5	.607	6.745	83.631				
6	.501	5.570	89.201				
7	.457	5.077	94.278				
8	.327	3.634	97.911				
9	.188	2.089	100.00				

Pattern Matrix		
	Factor	
	1	2
relig02 GOD WANTS TO BE OUR GOD	.921	
relig01 GOD IS CONCERNED WITH EVERY INDIVIDUAL PERSONALLY	.853	

Pattern Matrix

	Factor	
	1	2
relig03 LIFE HAS A MEANING BECAUSE OF THE EXISTENCE GOD	.773	
relig05 DEATH HAS A MEANING IF YOU BELIEVE IN GOD	.640	
relig04 BELIEF IN GOD CAN HELP US BEAR A LOT OF PAIN	.596	
con4 IT IS NOT NATURAL FOR A WOMAN TO SUPERVISE MEN		.739
con2 EDUCATION OF DAUGHTER IS LESS IMPORTANT THAN SON		.727
con3 BOYS ARE RAISED LESS STRICT THAN GIRLS		.563
con1 WOMEN ARE MORE FIT TO RAISE CHILDREN THAN MEN		.404

Factor Correlation Matrix

Factor	1	2
1	1.000	.368
2	.368	1.000

Descriptive Statistics

	N	Minimum	Maximum	Mean	Std. Deviation
FAC1_1	1667	−2.11498	1.47468	.000000	.95106077
FAC2_1	1667	−4.03862	1.21524	.000000	.87107022
Valid N (listwise)	1667				

4.13 RELIABILITY △

Function

The RELIABILITY command is used to determine whether multiple items are suitable to be used in a Likert scale. To determine scalability, correlations and Cronbach's α are used as measures of reliability.

Structure

RELIABILITY is followed by VARIABLES and the names of the variables included in the scale. STATISTICS CORRELATIONS checks whether all items correlate positively, which is a necessary condition for assessing the reliability. SUMMARY followed by TOTAL can be used to evaluate whether deleting an item increases or decreases Cronbach's α.

Example

```
RELIABILITY
 /VARIABLES RELIG01 TO RELIG05
 /STATISTICS CORRELATIONS
  /SUMMARY TOTAL.
COMPUTE SCALER = RELIG01 + RELIG02 + RELIG03 +
RELIG04 + RELIG05.
DESCRIPTIVES SCALER.
```

In this example, the Cronbach's α is calculated for a scale consisting of five items that all refer to religion (Table 4.12a). The change in Cronbach's α when an item is deleted from the scale is also calculated. The Likert scale is constructed using COMPUTE (p. 34) and displayed by DESCRIPTIVES (Table 4.12b). Please note that only respondents with a value on *all* five items are included in the analysis. MEAN.n may be specified instead (see p. 118), if too many cases are lost using the listwise deletion of missing scores.

Results

Table 4.12a   Cronbach's α of Religion Scale (RELIG1–5)

Reliability Statistics		
Cronbach's Alpha	**Cronbach's Alpha Based on Standardized Items**	**N of Items**
.871	.870	5

Table 4.12b Correlation Matrix, Means, Variances, and Cronbach's α If an Item Is Deleted and Descriptive Measures of the Final Likert Scale

Inter-Item Correlation Matrix		relig01	relig02	relig03	relig04	relig05
relig01	GOD IS CONCERNED WITH EVERY INDIVIDUAL PERSONALLY	1.000	.808	.672	.466	.498
relig02	GOD WANTS TO BE OUR GOD	.808	1.000	.705	.499	.552
relig03	LIFE HAS A MEANING BECAUSE GOD EXISTS	.672	.705	1.000	.468	.562
relig04	IF YOU BELIEVE IN GOD, YOU CAN BEAR A LOT OF PAIN	.466	.499	.468	1.000	.494
relig05	DEATH HAS A MEANING, IF YOU BELIEVE IN GOD	.498	.552	.562	.494	1.000

Item-Total Statistics					
	Scale Mean If Item Deleted	Scale Variance If Item Deleted	Corrected Item-Total Correlation	Squared Multiple Correlation	Cronbach's Alpha If Item Deleted
relig01	13.52	17.503	.760	.676	.828
relig02	13.51	16.807	.804	.716	.816
relig03	12.88	18.769	.742	.567	.834
relig04	13.52	20.485	.564	.330	.874
relig05	13.01	19.762	.626	.408	.861

Descriptive Statistics					
	N	Minimum	Maximum	Mean	Std. Deviation
SCALER	1695	5.00	25.00	16.6100	5.31561
Valid N (listwise)	1695				

△ 4.14 SPSS Syntax: An Overview

```
GET FILE "c:/Data/chapter4.sav".

*** 4.2: Describes variables.
DESCRIPTIVES YBIRTH LEAVECHURCH MOVEOUT
 /STATISTICS MEAN VARIANCE RANGE.

*** Saves z-scores.
DESCRIPTIVES YBIRTH (Z_YBIRTH) MOVEOUT (Z_MOVEOUT)
 /SAVE
 /MISSING LISTWISE.
DESCRIPTIVES Z_YBIRTH Z_MOVEOUT.

*** 4.3: Shows frequency distributions.
FREQUENCIES SEX EDUC.

*** Extensive Example.
FREQUENCIES SEX EDUC
 /FORMAT AFREQ LIMIT(7)
 /BARCHART
 /STATISTICS MINIMUM MAXIMUM MEAN STDDEV
 /MISSING INCLUDE.

*** 4.4: Creates cross tables.
CROSSTABS CHRISTP BY CHURCHMEMBER.

*** Creates cross tables: elaboration.
CROSSTABS CHRISTP BY CHURCHMEMBER
 /TABLES CHRISTP BY CHURCHMEMBER BY EDUC2
 /CELLS COLUMN COUNT EXPECTED
 /STATISTICS CHISQ PHI.

*** 4.5: shows numeric and graphic representation of variables.
EXAMINE YBIRTH
 /PLOT BOXPLOT.

*** 4.6: Creates graph with means (paste).
GRAPH
 /LINE(SIMPLE)=MEAN (CHURCHMEMBER) BY EDUC.

***4.7: Compares means.
MEANS YBIRTH BY SEX BY REGION.
```

```
*** 4.7: Extensive Example ANOVA test and test for linearity.
MEANS RELIGION BY EDUC
 /CELLS MEAN MIN MAX
 /STATISTICS LINEARITY.

***4.8: Tests means.
T-TEST TESTVAL 40
 /VARIABLES AGE.

T-TEST GROUPS MARITALSTAT (2 3)
 /VARIABLES AGE.

T-TEST PAIRS HOURSSON HOURSFATH.

***4.9: Calculates correlations.
CORRELATIONS LEAVECHURCH MOVEOUT.

CORRELATIONS WORKHOURS HOURSFATH HOURSMOTH
 /MISSING PAIRWISE
 /PRINT ONETAIL.

***4.10: Regression analysis.
REGRESSION
 /DEPENDENT RELIGION
 /METHOD ENTER AGE EDUC3 SEX.

REGRESSION
 /STATISTICS R ANOVA COEFF COLLIN
 /CRITERIA PIN(.10) POUT(.20)
 /DEPENDENT RELIGION
 /METHOD STEPWISE SEX EDUC3 AGE
   WORKHOURS
 /RESIDUALS OUTLIERS(SDRESID, MAHAL, COOK)
 /SAVE PRED (PREDICT)
 /SCATTERPLOT (*ZRESID, *PRED).
DESCRIPTIVES PREDICT.

***4.11: Logistic regression analysis.
LOGISTIC REGRESSION CHURCHMEMBER
 /METHOD ENTER AGE SEX.

LOGISTIC REGRESSION CHURCHMEMBER
/CONTRAST (CHURCH15) = INDICATOR(1)
/CONTRAST (EDUC) = INDICATOR(3)
```

```
/METHOD = BSTEP AGE SEX CHURCH15 EDUC
/CRITERIA = PIN(.10) POUT(.20) ITERATE(20) CUT(.5)
/SAVE = PRED(PRED).
GRAPH LINE=MEAN(PRED) by EDUC.

***4.12: Factor and component analysis.
FACTOR
 /VARIABLES RELIG01 TO RELIG05.

FACTOR
 /VARIABLES RELIG01 TO RELIG05 CON1 TO CON4
 /FORMAT SORT BLANK(.40)
 /CRITERIA FACTORS(2) /EXTRACTION PAF
 /ROTATION OBLIMIN
 /SAVE REG (ALL).
DESCRIPTIVES FAC1_1 FAC2_1.

***4.13: Reliability analysis.
RELIABILITY
 /VARIABLES RELIG01 TO RELIG05
 /STATISTICS CORRELATIONS
 /SUMMARY TOTAL.
COMPUTE SCALER = RELIG01 + RELIG02 + RELIG03 + RELIG04 +
 RELIG05.

DESCRIPTIVES SCALER.
```

Appendix I

Arithmetic Expressions

I.1 Introduction △

An arithmetic expression is a calculation or a formula to compute a new variable or a value based on a number of variables and/or values. The following are the basic operations:

**	Exponentiation
*	Multiplying
/	Dividing
+	Adding
−	Subtracting

These basic operations will be executed by SPSS in the order we presented in the table. So the expression "5 + 3 − 4 * 2" will result in "5 + (3 − (4 * 2))" = 0. IF you want (parts of) the expression to be executed in a different order, you can use parentheses. For example, the expression "(5 + 3 − 4) * 2" results in the value 8. The symbol "−" can also be used for (part of) the expression as a whole, resulting in a negative outcome. The expression − (5 + 3 − 4) * 2 then results in −8. When an operation or function (see next section) is executed on a missing value, the result (unless otherwise mentioned) is again a missing value.

I.2 Functions △

Besides the basic operations mentioned above, SPSS provides a number of functions that can be applied to arithmetic expressions. The general notation is to first specify the function and then place the variables on which the

▶ 117

function is to be executed between parentheses and divide by commas (!). As an example, we take the mean scores of respondents on the variables RELIG01 to RELIG05. You could use COMPUTE (p. 34), but in case of many "missings" you may find the function MEAN more convenient. The syntax will then read as follows: COMPUTE AVERR = MEAN (RELIG01, RELIG02, RELIG03, RELIG04, RELIG05). Compute AVERR = MEAN(RELIG01 to RELIG05) gives the same result. Some commonly used statistical functions are given below:

SUM(var, varx)	Calculates the sum score of a number of variables (var)
MEAN(var, varx)	Calculates the mean
SD(var, varx)	Calculates the standard deviation
VAR(var, varx)	Calculates the variance
MIN(var, varx)	Calculates the minimum
MAX(var, varx)	Calculates the maximum

With all of these functions, it is possible to add a period (.) and a number, for example, COMPUTE AVERR = MEAN.4(RELIG01, RELIG02, RELIG03, RELIG04, RELIG05). The number represents the number of valid values needed for a valid result. If this is not specified, the number is 1. Thus, the mean is calculated if at least one variable has a valid value. In the example above, four out of five variables should have a valid value, so one observation can be missing or invalid. In that case, SPSS calculates the mean using these four valid values. Some other commonly used functions are given below:

ABS(var)	Calculates the absolute value of scores on the var(iable)
SQRT(var)	Calculates the root from the score
EXP(var)	Calculates the score to the power of e (2.718)
LN(var)	Calculates the logarithm (base e) of the score
LG10(var)	Calculates the logarithm (base 10) of the score
RND(var)	Rounds every score to the nearest whole number
TRUNC(var)	Removes all decimals from the score

For example, COMPUTE NEW= LN (X) allows you to take the log transformation of a variable (X), as often used in variables that are skewed to the right. Certain calculations in SPSS will lead to "system missing," such as dividing by 0, taking the root from a negative value, exponentiation of a negative fraction, and calculating the logarithm from 0 or a negative value.

I.3 Limited Precision △

Computers are capable of performing complex calculations. However, each computer program stores and processes data in different ways. SPSS does this using "floating points" for precise results for very large as well as very small values. This leads to a number of potential problems. First, it is limited by the size of the values: if the value of the numbers is large, it results in "overflow" (SPSS will enter a "system missing" in this case); and if the value of the numbers is small, it results in "underflow" (SPSS will enter 0 in that case). Second, SPSS stores only approximate values. Values to the power of 2 are stored without error, but for other values, only the first 13 to 14 digits are stored. Finally, some calculations are more sensitive to precision than others. For example, if the number 3 is stored internally as 2.9999999999999999, TRUNC, IF, and RECODE may result in unexpected results. Therefore, it is recommended to round values beforehand with RND (see above).

Appendix II

Logical Expressions

Logical expressions contain statements. If the statement is true, the value 1 is attributed; if it is not, then 0. For example, in Section 3.17, the command COMPUTE MALE = (SEX = 1) is used. This means that all males score the value 1 on the variable MALE, because males are coded 1 on the variable SEX, so the statement SEX = 1 is true for males. Women (0 for SEX) get the value 0 for MALE, because the statement is not true for them. The following symbols and abbreviations are used in logical expressions:

Symbol		Abbreviation	Meaning
>	or	GT	Greater than
<	or	LT	Less than
=	or	EQ	Equal to
>=	or	GE	Greater than or equal to
<=	or	LE	Less than or equal to
<>	or	NE	Not equal to

SELECT IF YBIRTH > 1970 selects all respondents born after 1970, because the statement is true for them and only them. SELECT IF YBIRTH GT 1970 gives the same result. Generally, using abbreviations results in a more comprehensible syntax than using symbols.

△ II.2 Logic

There are three operations in SPSS that can be executed on logical values: (1) AND, (2) OR, and (3) NOT. These can also be represented by the symbols "&," "|," and "~," but we feel the name of the operator is easier to read than the symbol. The operators AND and OR are executed for all values that precede and follow the operator. NOT relates only to the value that follows the operator. The following table presents the results of the three operations:

A	B	A AND B (Results)	A	B	A OR B (Results)	A	NOT A (Results)
0	0	0	0	0	0	0	1
0	1	0	0	1	1	1	0
1	0	0	1	0	1		
1	1	1	1	1	1		

The value 0 represents the condition "not true"; the value 1 represents "true." You can use parentheses here as well to keep part of the expression together. The expression "((YBIRTH > 1970) AND (SEX = 1)) OR (CHURCHMEMBER = 1)" is true not only for all males born after 1970 but also for all church members. This means that males born after 1970 who are church members also comply with this statement. If the expression is used with the command SELECT IF, all women and men born before 1971 and disaffiliated are excluded from further data modifications and analyses. Please note that normal language sometimes differs from formal logic. When you state that "codes 4, 5, and 6 should become 1," the logical operation OR is to be used, because each observation can only be equal to one of these codes: IF (EDUC=4 OR EDUC=5 OR EDUC=6) EDUCCAT=1.

△ II.3 Functions

There are a number of functions in SPPS that produce logical values (see arithmetic expressions on p. 117 for a general explanation of the functions):

MISSING(var)	Is "true" if the score on the var(iable) is defined as invalid ("missing").
SYSMIS(var)	Is "true" if there is no score on the var(iable) (system-missing).
RANGE(var, number1, number2)	Is "true" if the score of the var(iable) is between number1 and number2 (or equal to).
ANY(var, row values)	Is "true" if the score on the variable is present in the mentioned row of values (divided by commas).

The use of MISSING and SYSMIS is intuitive. RANGE and ANY are used for brief statements. Instead of "YBIRTH >= 1950 AND YBIRTH <= 1960," you can use RANGE(YBIRTH, 1950, 1960). "VOTES = 2 OR VOTES = 6 OR VOTES = 7 OR VOTES = 8" becomes "ANY(VOTES, 2, 6, 7, 8)."

Index

⑤SAGE research**methods**

The essential online tool for researchers from the world's leading methods publisher

Find exactly what you are looking for, from basic explanations to advanced discussion

More content and new features added this year!

"I have never really seen anything like this product before, and I think it is really valuable."

John Creswell, University of Nebraska–Lincoln

Discover **Methods Lists**— methods readings suggested by other users

Watch video interviews with leading methodologists

Explore the **Methods Map** to discover links between methods

Search a custom-designed taxonomy with more than 1,400 qualitative, quantitative, and mixed methods terms

Uncover more than 120,000 pages of book, journal, and reference content to support your learning

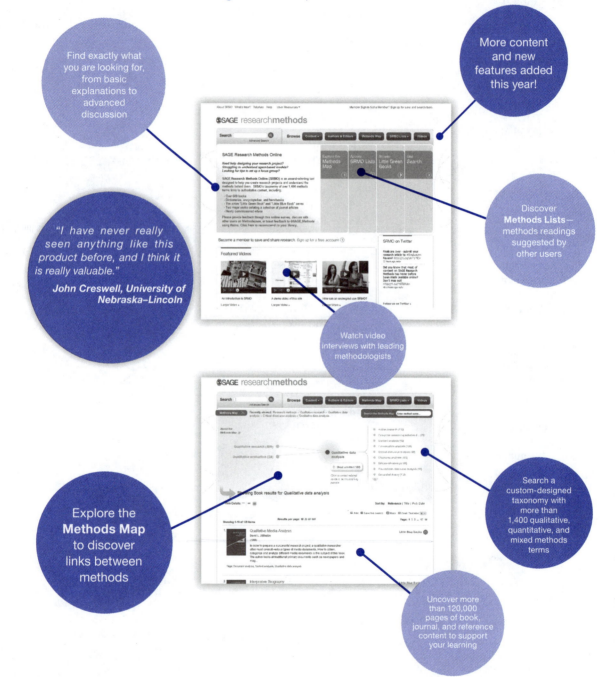

Find out more at
www.sageresearchmethods.com